Dorothy:

From
the Library
of

ROBERT CALDER WATSON
1912 - 1998

JB0-00094 © APCo.

TENEMENT
CASTLEBANK STREET
PARTICK.

THE
GLASGOW
TENEMENT

A WAY OF LIFE

AD MAJOREM GLORIAM DEI

To the memory of my mother, whose help and encouragement made this book possible.

THE GLASGOW TENEMENT

A WAY OF LIFE

A SOCIAL, HISTORICAL AND ARCHITECTURAL STUDY

FRANK WORSDALL

Chambers

First published 1979 by W& R Chambers Ltd
First paperback edition published 1989 by Richard Drew Publishing Ltd

This edition published 1991 by W & R Chambers Ltd,
43—45 Annandale Street, Edinburgh EH7 4AZ

British Library Cataloguing in Publication Data

A catalogue record for this book is
available from the British Library

ISBN 0-550-22561-7

Printed and bound in Great Britain by
Butler and Tanner Ltd, Frome, Somerset

Contents

List of Plates and Figures

Figures

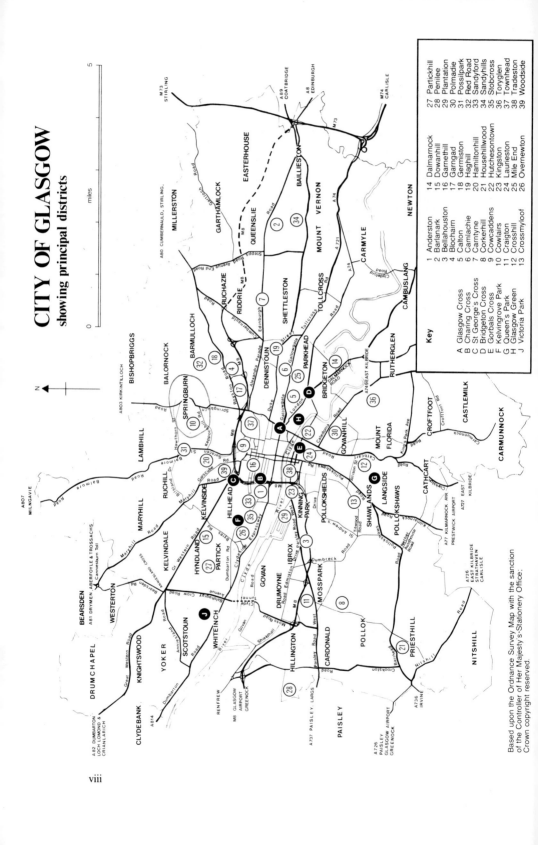

CITY OF GLASGOW
showing principal districts

N

0   miles   5

Key

A Glasgow Cross
B Charing Cross
C St George's Cross
D Bridgeton Cross
E Gorbals Cross
F Kelvingrove Park
G Queen's Park
H Glasgow Green
J Victoria Park

1 Anderston
2 Barlanark
3 Bellahouston
4 Blochairn
5 Calton
6 Camlachie
7 Carntyne
8 Corkerhill
9 Cowcaddens
10 Cowlairs
11 Craigton
12 Crosshill
13 Crossmyloof
14 Dalmarnock
15 Dowanhill
16 Garnethill
17 Garngad
18 Germiston
19 Haghill
20 Hamiltonhill
21 Househillwood
22 Hutchesontown
23 Kingston
24 Laurieston
25 Mile End
26 Overnewton
27 Partickhill
28 Penilee
29 Plantation
30 Polmadie
31 Possilpark
32 Red Road
33 Sandyford
34 Sandyhills
35 Stobcross
36 Toryglen
37 Townhead
38 Tradeston
39 Woodside

Introduction

The tenement is the traditional form of urban housing in Scotland, and it found its highest expression during the nineteenth century in Glasgow, in the great period of industrial expansion. Glasgow is a city of tenements. Their polished ashlar frontages of white and red stone have for centuries impressed visitors unused to such well-built housing. Unfortunately, as a result of various social and political pressures, large areas of the city have recently been demolished, without sufficient thought being given to the social and cultural loss which this was bound to entail. After all, not so many years ago, Glasgow could be described as the finest nineteenth-century city in Europe, and this solely on the quality of its architecture. That quality was not confined simply to public and commercial buildings, but also embraced the long street-vistas of tenement housing. It was in order to record the excellence of those buildings and the life which they represented that the author began the research which has made this book possible.

'Tenement' these days is a dirty word and is used almost exclusively to describe a slum property. It is this attitude of mind which has been responsible for the destruction of so much of our heritage — buildings which could, with a little foresight, have been reconstructed to provide continuing homes for their occupants. The policy of destruction, that something new is always better than something old, is wrong and can be clearly seen to be so in the vandalism, the lack of community spirit, the general hopelessness and helplessness of life in a high-rise flat or a monster housing scheme.

The word *tenementum* — Latin: 'a holding' — takes us back both to the Romans and the feudal system of the Middle Ages. The term originally referred to land and was synonymous with a steading, or plot of ground. With the passing of time the word came to mean the dwelling-house erected on the ground, no matter what its kind. By the nineteenth century it was used with reference only to a specific type of building, namely a domestic building of more than one story, all the houses of which are reached by a common entrance and stair. This is the definition which will be used throughout the book.

Preface

Since the first edition of this book appeared in 1979, attitudes towards tenement housing and the urban environment in general, has radically changed. The common post-war choice between a flat in a multi-storey block or one in a monster peripheral housing scheme, is now quite unacceptable. So is the wholesale destruction of the old communities and the friendly way of life they represent. Instead, people want to stay in their present familiar environment, with their homes brought up to modern standards, and this is now what is frequently happening.

Ten years on, the outlook is brighter than it was in the 1970s, and this is reflected in this new edition of 1989. The text has been brought up to date, and new photographs have been introduced. A number of improvements have been made, including the restoration of the original title. Previously the scope of the book — a study of tenement housing and its development within the city of Glasgow — was obscured.

I hope that, in its new form THE GLASGOW TENEMENT will be a source of both information and pleasure to those who have not come across it before.

BACKGROUND

1
The Social and Economic Background

Rome was the first civilisation to erect large numbers of buildings of more than one story — the Colosseum is perhaps the best known example and there is evidence to suggest that many-storied blocks of houses existed in crowded centres like the port of Ostia and in the city of Rome itself. These buildings, it would appear, formed dwellings for the poorer section of the urban population. Mediaeval society fostered the tall building divided into many separate dwellings as a convenient way of housing numerous families within a restricted area. The walled cities of Italy and France, in particular, forced a vertical approach to architectural problems on their master builders.

Such problems did not reach Scotland until the second half of the sixteenth century, when there was a considerable change in social conditions. There was a general increase in wealth, with better standards of living and a gradual, if guarded, interest in the arts. These improvements were to be found chiefly in the *burghs*, the communities which had special privileges of local and foreign trade. Glasgow, already a cathedral city, had been created a burgh by King William the Lion between 1175 and 1178.[1] Nevertheless, its position on the west coast militated against early development in an age when most trade was carried on from the east of the country, and it did not emerge as a significant trading port until the post-Reformation period.

The inhabitants of burghs were divided into two groups, burgesses and non-burgesses.[2] The former were subdivided into merchants and craftsmen, each belonging to a guild, and these two classes enjoyed all the burghal privileges to the exclusion of all the other inhabitants. The merchants were socially and politically the more important, having the extra privilege of foreign trade with the wealth and prestige which that brought. Thus they usually dominated the burgh's ruling body, the town council. In Glasgow, however, merchants and craftsmen were almost equally represented on the council — an unusual situation, because the two bodies did not generally regard each other as equals.[3]

Entrance to the merchants' guild was by apprenticeship and thereafter by the payment of a fee, graded according to the status of the applicant. Merchants' sons were privileged and paid the lowest fee, while many other apprentices found it convenient to marry their master's daughter in order to avoid the extremely large sum demanded of those outside the merchant class.[4]

Trade in seventeenth-century Scotland was very broadly-based. Goods exported by the Glasgow merchants included wool, linen and coal, with wine, timber or paper being carried on the return voyage. Specialised cargoes did not become common until the following century. The ports most frequented by Scottish ships were Rotterdam, Danzig, Stockholm, Bordeaux and London, and many merchants found it convenient to spend some years in one of these places. On returning home, besides their new wealth they also brought a knowledge of cultured European society to enrich Scottish burgh life. There is no doubt that the merchant was materially and culturally better-off than any other class except the nobility.

Unlike the merchants, with their single incorporation, the craftsmen organised themselves into a number of trade guilds. By 1600, Glasgow had fourteen of these; the Hammermen, Tailors, Cordiners, Maltmen, Weavers, Baxters, Skinners, Wrights, Masons, Coopers, Fleshers, Gardeners, Barbers, and Bonnetmakers and Dyers.[5] The total membership of the craft guilds, or *Trades House* as it came to be called, was 361. Entry to a craft guild was similar to that for the merchants' — by means of apprenticeship (which could last for up to seven years) and the payment of an entry fee.[6]

As for the other inhabitants of the burghs, the non-burgesses, little is known, for most of them have left no record of their lives or activities. They consisted mainly of the poor and labouring classes, but also included such other members of the community as members of the legal profession, who did not fit into the accepted burgess-class by right.

The pattern of urban development in sixteenth-century Scotland in many respects resembled that elsewhere along the coastline of Europe. Land for building was at a premium in the larger coastal trading towns and therefore, for purely practical reasons, it was found necessary to build upward. It must be remembered that the burgh boundaries had been laid down long before this date, and were immovable. The burgesses were obliged to maintain the town wall (if there was one) and the *ports* or gates, and to make certain that no one could gain admittance to the burgh through their property. Glasgow had probably as many as eleven ports at various times, each strategically placed on one of the roads leading into the city from the north, east and west, and also at the important entrance from the bridge over the Clyde on the south. Within, the buildings along the main streets rose gradually higher and higher, reaching the height of three stories and attic by 1600.[7]

The biggest drawback to the expansion of trade was the shallowness of the River Clyde, which allowed only small craft to reach the city.[8] To overcome this handicap, in the second half of the seventeenth century, when trade with the New World was beginning to assume vital importance, a new harbour and township were established eighteen miles downstream at Newark, later called New Port or Port Glasgow.[9] The river was in its natural silted-up state until almost a century later, when the engineer John Golborne of Chester was called in to advise on, and superintend, the work of river-deepening. In 1774, some primitive dredging was carried out and a stone embankment erected for about ten miles along the south side of the river.[10] This deepened it from the natural 2 feet to 6 ft 10 in.[11]

Free trade with the English colonies was legalised by the Treaty of Union of 1707, when the Scottish and English parliaments were merged. Almost immediately, the west coast became the centre of trade with the American colonies and Glasgow began to rival Bristol in importance. The shrewd Glasgow merchants imported tobacco, rum, mahogany and raw cotton from America and exported cargoes of linen cloth and thread, gloves, shoes and hats, all of which found a ready market in the colonies. Those strutting grandees, the Glasgow Tobacco Lords, in their scarlet cloaks, powdered wigs and tricorn hats, were symptomatic of the radical changes of thought and fashion which were sweeping the city. For the first time we find a cultural exchange with England, the old enemy. If the Jacobite risings of 1715 and 1745 emphasised differences in religious and political loyalties, the lack of support they elicited in Lowland Scotland served to show the general contentment which the majority of people in the United

3

Kingdom were beginning to feel under Hanoverian rule.

In his *History of Glasgow*, published in 1777, John Gibson, himself a merchant, provides invaluable tables of the import and export trade of the city for the year 1771, clearly showing how lucrative it had become. Apart from the American colonies, there was regular trade with Italy, Spain, Portugal, France, Holland, Poland, Sweden, Russia, Norway and Ireland. Imports included salted beef, timber, Irish linen, lemons, sugar and rum (the ingredients of the famous Glasgow punch!) as well as tobacco. Exports included glass, linen, candles, handkerchiefs, pottery and wool, as well as the re-export of sugar and tobacco.[12]

At first, the merchants of that period were content to live in the tenements which had become the traditional form of urban housing but, as they began to amass great wealth, their ideas of comfort underwent a change. They began to purchase ground outside the boundaries of the old city-burgh on which to build their new homes, which were quite different from anything which had been built by their predecessors — a simplified form of Italian Renaissance villa, with pediments, Corinthian pilasters, Palladian windows, balustrades and ornamental urns. Many of these were built in a New Town to the west of the old city and the names given to the streets, 'Virginia' and 'Jamaica' for example, are indicative of the source of Glasgow's new-found wealth.[13] In 1775, when the tobacco trade came to a sudden end with the outbreak of the American War of Independence, the effects were not as disastrous as might have been anticipated. The merchants' great fortunes had already been made and they simply transferred their trade to the West Indies.

While all this was going on in Glasgow, the cotton industry had begun in Lancashire. Following the invention of the Spinning Jenny (1765), the Water-Frame (1769) and the Spinning Mule (1779), conditions were right for its introduction into the Clyde valley. Renfrewshire and Lanarkshire were ideal for the purpose owing to the abundance of water power, the availability of labour, the close proximity to a large city for distribution, and a number of ports for the reception of the raw cotton. David Dale, the most important of the post-tobacco merchants, with the advice of Richard Arkwright, the inventor of the Water-Frame, founded the most famous of the spinning-mills, New Lanark, in 1784.[14] Work began two years later and a village was built beside the mills. The houses were built in three-storied stone tenement blocks, much closer to contemporary town architecture than to that of the countryside. This was the first Scottish industrial housing, and as such was to have a considerable influence on future developments.[15]

With the application of steam power to cotton spinning, there was an immediate concentration of mills in the area just outside the city limits. In 1787 there were nineteen mills there; in 1796, thirty-nine. The next few years were the period of greatest expansion, resulting in a total of 120 mills by 1812. The chief centres of the industry were Anderston on the west and the Calton on the east. These two rural villages rapidly changed character following the erection of so many mills and assumed the importance of industrial communities. Being outwith the city — and therefore beyond the control, however slight, of the authorities there — the standard of housing tended to be poor. Three-storied tenements, often of brick with scant provision for comfort, were packed as close to one another, and to the mill, as could be managed.[16] The Calton in particular retained something of its old character until as late as the 1920s, when the centre of the village was swept away under an Improvement Scheme.

Where did the work-force to run this vast new industrial complex come from? Starving droves of people, displaced by the clearances in Ireland and the Scottish highlands, came from impoverished crofts and unwillingly worked in the factories; ploughmen left the fields for the mills and farmers were forced eventually to raise their wages in an attempt to keep workers in their service. Gradually, however, as the mill machinery changed — particularly after the introduction of the power-loom and mechanised weaving — so the labour force changed to a predominantly female one. Children, of course, had always been employed and this use of child labour was one of the strongest criticisms levelled against the mill-owners. There were obvious advantages in using small children to crawl under the machinery to sweep away fluff during spinning, and many owners believed that only those 'caught' before the age of twelve could ever be trained to become first-class workers in their later years.

David Dale, kind and godly man as he was, brought hundreds of orphan children to work at New Lanark, where they toiled for twelve hours a day with an hour's break for food. He accommodated them in a special building where they slept in 'well-aired rooms, three in a bed, on a straw mattress with sheets and blankets, the dormitories being scrubbed weekly and lime-washed twice a year'. Even after work their lives were regulated. They had to attend the factory school for two hours. Food consisted of oatmeal porridge with milk twice a day and, for lunch, soup with barley bread and potatoes, then meat, herrings or bread and cheese. Dale's benevolent use of child labour was greatly admired, but not frequently emulated.[17] However, when his son-in-law Robert Owen took over the mills in 1799, he began twenty-five years of educational and cooperative experiment there which astonished the industrial world.[18]

In and around Glasgow things were different. The mill-workers were not segregated as in the rural areas, but drawn from the district around their place of employment. In the 1820s a spinner in a Glasgow factory, particularly if he had two or three children in their teens, could be quite well off. He could earn £1 per week, with his children contributing another 7s or 8s a week to the family budget. His home frequently consisted of a two-apartment rented tenement flat containing a table, chairs, a chest of drawers, a mahogany bedstead, a well-stocked china cabinet and some books. A status symbol was provided by the grandfather clock, which was capable of looking splendid even if its works were in the pawnshop.[19]

Inevitably, many of the thousands who flocked to the city in the early years of the nineteenth century were unable to find work. These, added to the people made unemployed by serious recessions of trade in 1816, 1819 and 1826, when the mills closed their doors, meant that there were large numbers of people in great poverty, able to afford only the most wretched accommodation. They congregated, as immigrant communities tend to do, in the oldest parts of the city — the High Street with its wynds, the Gallowgate, Bridgegate and Saltmarket — where buildings were oldest and rents cheapest. To take advantage of this wretched market and the lack of legislation to safeguard health, tenements of the poorest description were built in what had been garden ground belonging to the street buildings. These *back-lands* — *land* being an old synonym for *tenement* — were reached only by narrow lanes or closes, which meant that they were deficient in both light and ventilation. Needless to say, the poverty-stricken inhabitants contributed nothing in the way of care or maintenance of these buildings and they quickly deteriorated into the most wretched slums.

A good idea of conditions in those areas in the mid-nineteenth century can be obtained from the photographs taken by Thomas Annan, from 1868 onwards, of many of the buildings just before their removal. (See Plates 3, 4 and 5.) These photographs were commissioned and later published by the City Improvement Trust as a record of their work.[20] Particularly noticeable are the narrow paved or cobbled lanes with an open drain down one side and the conglomeration of buildings, part domestic and part industrial, which had grown up over the previous century. One of the features of these old photographs is the quantity of astonishingly shapeless washing suspended on poles projecting from upper-floor windows! One particularly bad specimen of a 'jerry-built' tenement unfortunately does not appear in any photograph or drawing. This was the notorious 'Rookery' in the Drygate, where, in a single close, no fewer than five hundred persons claimed a dwelling.

The final incentive for the long-overdue measures to improve the city's slum areas was provided by the cholera epidemics which occurred in 1848–9 and 1853–4, causing the death of 3772 and 3885 persons respectively. These epidemics were largely caused by a defective water supply, and a committee was set up in 1857 to examine the whole question of public health and how conditions could be improved. The opening of the Loch Katrine Water Scheme three years later, with the introduction of pure water instead of that taken from the Clyde and a number of contaminated wells, played an important part in the improvement.

In 1859 another committee was appointed, this time to examine the question of sanitary legislation and to report on conditions in other large cities in the British Isles. One of the members of this committee was John Carrick, later first City Architect, whose influence on all decisions was considerable. On 25 October the committee reported that they had visited the old town and found that almost every spare inch of ground had been built upon, so that room could not be found to lay down an ash-pit. Buildings had been increased in height, with separate families in every apartment, until the place appeared to teem with inhabitants. The water supply was still defective and in many cases non-existent. The report continues:

> But bad as is the condition of the older districts of the city, a worse state of matters was disclosed by an inspection of some of the more recently-erected houses for the working-classes. . . . Tenements of great height are ranged on either side of narrow lanes with no back-yard space, and are divided from top to bottom into numberless small dwellings all crowded with occupants. The atmosphere of such houses is, to a stranger, oftentimes unbearable, and is rendered more pestilential by the presence of water-closets in the ill-ventilated lobbies or staircases of the building.

The committee then recommended

> That power be obtained to regulate the erection of new buildings, in order that the height of such buildings may be preserved proportionate to the width of the streets, lanes, courts, and closes in which they may be built. That the

dimensions of the apartments be not too small, and ... due regard be paid to light and ventilation. That it be rendered compulsory that such buildings have ample ash-pit and water-closet or privy accommodation. That owners of houses be obliged to provide a sufficient water-supply to their tenements.

The committee also recommended that baths and wash-houses for the use of the working-classes should be erected throughout the city.[21]

This enquiry resulted in the Police Act of 1862 and the setting up of the City Improvement Trust in 1866. (See page 23) Unfortunately, when drastic action was ultimately taken for the improvement of the old city, not only were the slum properties removed but also the University buildings in the High Street, the picturesque castle and mansion house in the Gorbals and the seventeenth-century buildings in the Saltmarket and Bridgegate, including the last of the half-timbered houses.

One of the methods employed by the Improvement Trust was the erection of common lodging-houses, or 'models' as they were generally known.[22] These were intended to cater for the needs of what were called 'the dregs of the population', who had previously found shelter in the numerous lodging-houses scattered through the wynds and vennels. A report of 1896 tells us that the normal inmate of the lodging-house has no place in the social scale and no desire to attain one. 'His horizon extends not beyond the day to which he awakens, and if for that day he can stay the pangs of hunger, if he can get wherewithal to command the two luxuries of his life — alcohol and tobacco — therewith he is content.'

Seven lodging-houses were built between 1871 and 1884. The smallest, in Greendyke Street by Glasgow Green, had 246 beds, while the largest, in Portugal Street in the Gorbals, had accommodation for 437. The 'motley multitude' who inhabited them seldom owned more than the clothes in which they presented themselves, and the coppers with which to secure a night's shelter. 'They are of all nationalities, ... disrobed clergymen and street bullies, decayed gentlemen and area sneaks, tramps, tinkers, labourers, sweeps, thieves, and thimble-riggers. The moral tone is low, the habits are generally unclean, and so sometimes is the language.'[23]

For 3d or 4½d per night not much could be expected. Each lodger, however, had a separate cubicle in a large dormitory divided by wooden partitions seven feet high, and a comfortable bed with daily-aired and weekly-changed bedclothes. The lodger had to be out of the dormitory by 8 am, but had the use of the rest of the establishment for twenty-four hours. There was a kitchen with a hotplate, cooking utensils and dishes, a commodious dining-hall and recreation rooms. In addition there was a shop which sold uncooked food, and, of course, bath and lavatory accommodation. There were drawbacks, however. The superintendents were ex-military men specially chosen to enforce discipline, and the police looked in regularly on Saturday nights. Free bibles, regular religious services and improving lectures were provided in a vain attempt to solve a humanitarian problem which is still with us.

One step up the social scale were the inhabitants of 'farmed houses'. Again quoting from the report of 1896:

> As the common lodging-house represents the hotel of the very poor, so the farmed house takes the place of the furnished apartments of the better-circumstanced citizens. The farmed house is taken from week to week by a class of people too poor to afford even the scanty outfit which goes to furnish the apartments they hire. ... The speculators, who themselves dwell amid the scene of their activity, rent entire tenements or blocks, each separate room of which they fit out with a bed or beds, some bedding, a table, two or three chairs, a grate, a kettle and pot, and a little crockery, and therewith each room becomes a 'furnished house'. Such houses are let to the unfortunate and improvident at rents ranging from 4/– per week upwards. ... The rooms are generally occupied by couples, with or without families, and although in the majority of instances one couple only was found in occupation, there were cases found of from two to four couples sleeping in the same apartment.[24]

In a determined attempt to prevent overcrowding, the system of 'ticketing' houses was evolved in 1866. All houses of three apartments or less and not exceeding 2000 cubic feet were measured, and their capacity, along with the number of occupants allowed by law — at the rate of 300 cubic feet for every person over eight years old — was inscribed on a metal plate which was fixed to the door. (See Plate 6.) By the 1880s, Glasgow possessed 23 228 ticketed houses, of which 16 413 were single apartments. About 75 000 people, one seventh of the city's population, occupied these houses.

The ticketed house was liable to a visit without warning during the night from the sanitary inspectors, whose duty it was to enforce the law regarding the number of occupants. One inspector in the Calton district reported that he had found people in every conceivable corner of the house — in cupboards, under beds and even on the housetop. In one case he found eleven adults in the house and seven more who had taken refuge on the roof — and that in a dwelling of only 880 cubic feet and therefore only fit for three persons. On another occasion he found two tiers of people in the same bed, one on the mattress and the other among the bedclothes above.[25]

The general decay of the old centres of population and the great spread of working-class housing which had, by the latter part of the century, engulfed the previously 'genteel' areas, caused the inhabitants of those areas to look for houses elsewhere. By 1850, fashions had changed and in order to cater for the new ideas a different kind of development began to appear. This was the garden suburb — self-contained cottages or villas with a third or half an acre of ground, built within a pleasant and carefully safeguarded semi-rural environment. The most successful of these suburbs were Pollokshields in the south-west, Dennistoun in the east and Kelvinside and Dowanhill in the north-west. The tenement, however, still retained its place as the traditional building-type and expensive, high-class schemes were begun about the same time at Garnethill and in the west at St Vincent Crescent and Sandyford.

City expansion reached its height during the boom years 1872–6, when no fewer than 21 052 tenement houses were authorised by the Dean of Guild Court. This was the period when the long streets of Dalmarnock, Govanhill, Springburn and Maryhill were laid out and the repetitive elevations of working-class tenements began to dominate the Glasgow scene. As might be expected, this boom period was followed by one of recession, culminating in the failure of the City of Glasgow Bank in 1878. This was a disastrous event for the building industry, as the City Bank's special interest had been the financing of builders and the encouragement of speculative development. In the winter following the collapse, 14 000 people in the city applied for poor relief which, taking dependants into account, meant that the number of destitute had reached the appalling figure of about 40 000. Architecturally, the results of the failure could long be seen in the form of many unfinished housing developments. Nevertheless, such was the resilience of the city at that period that by the mid-1880s the building trade had almost fully recovered from the blow, and the next twenty years were relatively prosperous, with new residential districts such as Hyndland, Battlefield and Langside being built.

By 1910, however, legislation made it uneconomical for private builders to continue building houses for rent and the erection of tenements virtually ceased. The City Improvement Trust rebuilt two blocks of old property in Rutherglen Road, Hutchesontown, but that was all. Ideas were changing once more and the middle classes, occupying their suburban villas, were being copied by their less wealthy brethren. The age of the semi-detached and the bungalow had arrived, and from then on it was to the building of these that the private builder turned his attention.

At the end of the First World War, responsibility for working-class housing was transferred to the local authority. The problem was magnified by the necessity of providing homes for the 'returning heroes', who were looking forward to the 'brave new world' they had been promised. What they wanted were pleasant, cottage-like houses with a small garden, set in attractive surroundings.[26] In an effort to provide just these ideals, the newly-formed Corporation Housing Department began work in 1920 on the first of the garden-suburbs, Riddrie, and quickly followed it with others at Mosspark and Knightswood.[27]

The idyllic new world of which these suburbs were to have been the forerunners never came about, however. Depression set in, and the Corporation were forced by overwhelming economic and social pressure to turn their attention to cheaper forms of housing. They produced a new stereotyped form of tenement, three stories in height, with houses of three, four or five apartments — no single-ends — but often, unfortunately, faced with artificial stone. These are to be found in nearly all the schemes undertaken during the 1920s and 1930s.

The period of almost total inactivity during the 1939–1945 war meant that the problem of rehousing had become even more acute by the time that hostilities ceased. Quite apart from the damage caused by bombing, the majority of houses in the city were now around a century old and had suffered from thirty years of neglect. The Corporation therefore considered it necessary to plan comprehensive redevelopment schemes covering practically the whole of the Victorian housing areas. Some of these — Hutchesontown, Laurieston and Pollokshaws, for example — have already been put into effect, and mass demolition is in progress preparatory to work beginning on a number of others. Such redevelopment however, is by its very nature a slow business, and other quicker methods of rehousing were required.

Chief among these alternative methods was the erection of monster housing estates on the periphery of the city, the best known of which

11

are Castlemilk, Drumchapel and Easterhouse, on the south, north and east respectively. No one can pretend that these schemes have been a success.[28] Although the overall planning was carefully thought out, the architectural standard of the houses, mostly tenements, is deplorable. The failure to provide adequate facilities has also caused much criticism, and the resulting general dissatisfaction has been blamed for the vandalism which is particularly noticeable in these districts.

In the 1950s and 1960s a new policy, that of housing in multi-story blocks, was accepted by the Corporation, and as a result the city landscape has been radically changed and now presents a picture little different from many other European cities. Despite the provision of lifts as well as staircases, these blocks are essentially tenements, continuing the old tradition in a new and extreme form. They have with justification been criticised for their tendency to dehumanise their occupants, and also to magnify social problems. The elderly, the infirm and those with young families have suffered particularly from this type of housing. Add to this the expensive nature of their construction, and there would seem to be powerful arguments for a return to a more traditional form of house-building.

The provision of satisfactory housing has been a major problem in our cities for many years, and unfortunately has frequently become a political issue. This does not ensure the best results. In Glasgow the policy during the 1960s and 70s was one of systematic destruction. The hearts of many of the old communities were torn out, followed by insensitive and soulless rebuilding leaving huge areas of dereliction where once the Victorian industries had flourished. Since 1979 attitudes have changed and the value of the tenement as a practical and efficient urban building form has once again been generally accepted. New tenements have been built, generally three stories in height, by both the District Council and private builders, the latter returning to the city centre after an absence of over 60 years. In addition, some areas have been revitalised, the old tenements refurbished, and something of the old community spirit restored. Although demolitions still occur, greater thought is being given to the provision of an attractive environment, and as a result the general appearance of the city is vastly improved. So, one hopes, is the quality of life.

1 The first impetus to the city's growth and importance was provided by Bishop John Cameron (1426–1446), who reorganised his Cathedral Chapter into thirty-two canons or prebends, each of whom was obliged to reside within the city for a considerable part of

each year. The canons built their manses along the Drygate and the Rottenrow, thus substantially increasing the city's size. J Primrose, *Mediaeval Glasgow* (1913) p 72.

2 A good account of burgh life and organisation is given in T C Smout, *A History of the Scottish People 1560–1830* (Collins 1969) p 146.
3 R Miller and J Tivy (eds), *The Glasgow Region* (1958) p 140.
4 Smout, p 153.
5 G Crawfurd, *A Sketch of the Rise and Progress of the Trades' House of Glasgow* (1858) p 46.
6 Smout, p 160.
7 One tenement, described in Chapter 6, bore the date 1596.
8 J D Marwick, *The River Clyde and the Clyde Burghs* (1909) p 46.
9 J Cleland, *Abridgement of the Annals of Glasgow* (1817) p 28.
10 G Crawfurd and W Semple, *The History of the Shire of Renfrew* (1782) p 60, where the primitive methods used are described.
11 Cleland, *Abridgement of the Annals* p 372.
12 J Gibson, *The History of Glasgow from the Earliest Accounts to the Present Time* (1777) p 213.
13 J F S Gordon (ed), *Glasghu facies — a View of the City of Glasgow* (2 vols, 1872) vol 2, p 1027.
14 For an account of Dale, see G Stewart, *Curiosities of Glasgow Citizenship* (1881) p 45.
15 Chapter on New Lanark, by J R Hume, in J Butt (ed), *Robert Owen, Prince of Cotton Spinners* (David and Charles 1971).
16 J E Handley, *The Irish in Scotland 1798–1845* (2nd ed 1964) p 281.
17 Smout, p 382.
18 See Butt, *Robert Owen*.
19 Smout, p 387.
20 T Annan, *Photographs of the Old Closes and Streets of Glasgow 1868–1877* (New ed, Dover Publications 1977).
21 'Senex' and others, *Glasgow past and present* (3 vols, 1884) vol I, p xxi.
22 For an excellent and detailed account of this subject, see S Laidlaw, *Glasgow Common Lodging-Houses and the People Living in Them* (1956).
23 J Bell and J Paton, *Glasgow, its Municipal Organization and Administration* (1896) p 192.
24 *ibid* p 194.
25 John Butt's chapter on 'Working-class housing in Glasgow 1851–1914', in S D Chapman (ed), *The History of Working-class housing — a Symposium* (1971) p 68ff, is full of interesting information on the subject.
26 T Brennan, *Reshaping a City — Glasgow* (1959) p 30.
27 *ibid* p 13.
28 *ibid* p 40.

2
The Legal Background

Roman Law and the Feudal System

When the tenement, in the form we recognise it, became common in Scotland in the latter half of the sixteenth century, those responsible for its erection faced few legal restrictions. There already existed a system of law sufficiently advanced for it to adapt its precepts to cover new types of housing and the problems of urban growth.

The law of the tenement was developed by the Burgh Court, and also by the Dean of Guild Court held under the auspices of the Merchants' House. The jurisdiction of these courts covered all buildings and, in addition, that ambiguous but widely-used term, 'local nuisances'. This eventually included such diverse things as defective drains, a badly-ventilated room or the presence of a smoking factory chimney.[1] The principles applied by the courts were simply those of good-neighbourliness and the *servitudes* of the Roman Law.

Some of these servitudes of the civil law were applied to building, but not inflexibly. If the servitude *altius non tollendi* (a person's right to prevent a neighbour from building higher than previously, to the detriment of the former's light or view) had been enforced, no tenement could ever have been built. The courts did, however, accept the servitude *tigni immitendi* (the right to use an adjacent proprietor's wall to support one's own building), and

14

developed it to permit a proprietor to build the end gables half on his own and half on his neighbour's ground. The latter then had the right to utilise this common gable for his joists and flues, on payment of half the cost.[2] In time it became customary for the first builder always to provide the outer side of his gables with fireplace-openings and chimney-vents ready for use by the adjacent proprietor. Many such gables may be seen throughout the city where, for one reason or another, they have remained unused.

The novel problems created by the ownership, not of a whole building, but of only a floor or even part of a floor, were solved by reference to the servitude *oneris ferendi* (the right to have one's property carried on top of someone else's). This gradually developed into a code of law particularly applicable to the tenement, evolved under the influence of the Burgh and Dean of Guild Courts. The main provisions of this code were as follows:

A The ground underneath the tenement, with any attached ground at the front or back, is the property of the ground-floor proprietor. The upper proprietors, however, have a common interest to prevent any use of it which would interfere with their light, etc.

B The horizontal division of the property is the centre line of the joists.

C The walls between two of these lines are the property of the flat proprietor, who is obliged to maintain them for the benefit of the other occupiers of the building.

D The roof is the property of the top-floor proprietor, but he may not add another full story.

E The common passage and stairs are the property of all the owners.

The earliest sixteenth- and seventeenth-century tenements would appear to have been built for mixed use, with shops or stores on the ground floor and dwelling-houses above. They were built for occupation by a number of different proprietors, each occupying one floor, part of a floor, or occasionally two floors. These proprietors were the burgesses — the merchants and craftsmen — who formed the special closed society of the burgh, as described in Chapter 1.

Mediaeval society in Scotland was organised under the feudal system, by which all power was attached to the possession of land. Grants of land had to come in the first place from the king, who was theoretically the owner or superior of the whole kingdom. He gave grants of land to his barons and knights, in that way ensuring their loyalty and also providing himself with an army, for military service was the chief return which such vassals made. When lands were given to the Church, the return took the form of perpetual prayers and supplications on the king's behalf.

King William the Lion's charter of *circa* 1175 granted 'to God and Saint Kentigern and to Joceline, Bishop of Glasgow, and to each of his successors for ever, to have a burgh at Glasgow with a market on Thursday, ... with all the freedoms and customs which any of my burghs in my whole land ... has'. This made Glasgow a *Burgh of Barony*, which was a community with a corporation subject to a feudal overlord, or *superior*. In this case, the superior was the bishop.[3]

In 1450, King James II raised Glasgow's status to that of a *Burgh of Regality*, in which the Crown retained only the right to deal with the crime of treason. The return was to be an annual payment

> by ... William and his successors, bishops of the Church of Glasgow, to me and my successors of a red rose at the Feast of the Nativity of Saint John the Baptist [24 June] at Glasgow, in name of blench farm, if asked, and the offering of devout prayers.[4]

The next step in the city's advancement was its promotion to the rank of a *Royal Burgh* by King James VI in 1611. This made a considerable administrative difference, for in a Royal Burgh the appointment of the town council was in the hands of the burgesses, instead of in those of the bishop as had been the case heretofore. The burgesses now held their lands *ex officio* — directly from the king — in return for the duty of 'watching and warding', *ie* guarding in the king's interest.[5]

The economic advantage of being a burgess was the enjoyment of a monopoly of trade within the burgh (except on market days) and, of course, all foreign trade. As a condition of this privilege, the merchants and craftsmen were required to reside, or at least have their places of business, within the burgh, the area of which was clearly defined. The ancient boundaries of the baronial burgh of Glasgow would appear to have been the River Clyde on the south, Saint Enoch's Burn on the west and north, and the Molendinar Burn on the east. These natural barriers may have been thought sufficient for defensive as well as for demarcation purposes, for the city never seems to have been enclosed by a wall, as a number of other burghs certainly were.[6] The ports, or gates, were all placed a considerable distance inside the actual boundary, so that the area of the city proper was relatively small.[7]

When a burgh's elected officials gave grants of land, the new owner held that land directly under the Crown in free *burgage* 'for services of burgh use and wont'. Outside burghs, land was held for various returns acknowledging the link with the superior or grantor. These returns originally took the form of services, but with the passing of

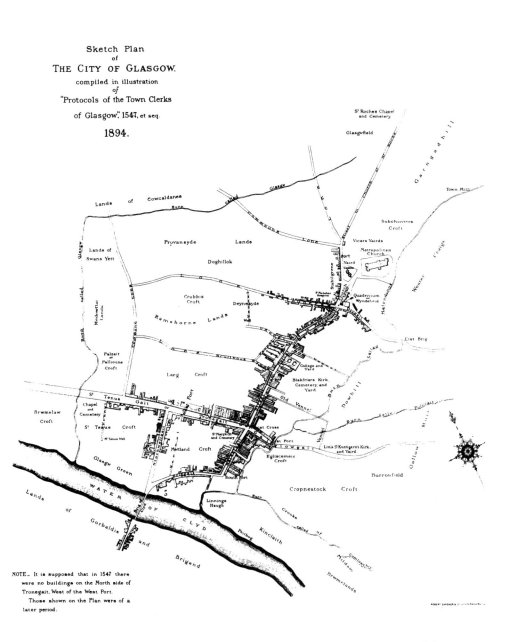

Sketch Plan
of
THE CITY OF GLASGOW.
compiled in illustration
of
"Protocols of the Town Clerks
of Glasgow", 1547, et seq.

1894.

NOTE — It is supposed that in 1547 there
were no buildings on the North side of
Tronegait, West of the West Port.
Those shown on the Plan were of a
later period.

Plate 1 Sketch plan of the City of Glasgow in the late sixteenth century. Many of the names are still recognisable although the burns, the ancient boundaries, are no longer visible.

Plate 2 A view of Glasgow from the south-west, 1767. On the right can be seen St Andrew's Parish Church, still without the surrounding square, and in the middle distance, on the nearer bank of the Clyde, is the old Gorbals village.

Plate 3 Annan: The Nightingale Close, 28 Saltmarket, *c* 1860. The building on the right is a timbered tenement of the late sixteenth or early seventeenth century. The upper story projects beyond the original stone building and the infill appears to be of plastered board.

Plate 4 Annan: The Pawn Close, 80 High Street 1868. Notice the outside sink at a first-floor window of the brick tenement on the right. It is noticeable that the close, although primitive, is considerably cleaner than a modern city street (see Plate 51).

Plate 5 Annan: The Fiddler's Close, 75 High Street. The photograph is an interesting illustration of the development of the city's water-supply: a pump above the original well can be seen in the right foreground, with behind it an outside sink at the top of the stairs—a transitional stage. In the tenement on the left there is an internal water-supply, although the soil-pipe still discharges into an open drain.

Plate 6 (above) 'Ticketed house' tokens. Each of these 3-inch discs gives the cubic footage of the house in question and the number of adults who could legally occupy it. 'Half an adult' can be interpreted as meaning a child under eight years of age. (*From the collection of the People's Palace, Glasgow Green.*)

Plate 7 (below) The impressive Greek portico of the recently refurbished Clarendon Place at Saint George's Cross, part of an ambitious housing project of 1839.

Plate 8 (right) The unified street elevation of Parliamentary Road. Although ranges of tenements, when viewed from the front, often appear to have been built as a unit, the back elevation is frequently far less uniform.

Plate 9 (upper left) The Palazzo della Cancelleria in Rome. The treatment of the second-floor windows is echoed in tenements all over Glasgow.

Plate 10 (left) A two-storey tenement in old Bridgeton. Notice the circular outside stair, the forerunner of the stair-towers of Plate 14.

Plate 11 (above) No 28 Stockwell Street, the last 17th century tenement to survive into modern times.

Plate 12 Cart-entrance—a pend at 47 Elmfoot Street. The opposite pend allowed ample access to the workshops in the back court.

Plate 13 A high-class 'wally close' of the 1890s in Glencairn Drive, Pollokshields. The stair-window is of painted glass.

Plate 14   *(upper left)* The impressive stair-towers at the back of Abbotsford Place.

Plate 15   *(left)* The 'minimum requirement' — Bridgeton. A privileged first-floor convenience.

Plate 16   *(above)* The back elevation of the fire-station buildings, Nicholson Street (see page 34). It is noticeable that a hundred years of 'progress' since the days of Thomas Annan have made little difference to the shapelessness of Glasgow's washing!

Plate 17 Ceiling-centre of the dining-room of a house at No 129 John Street. The tenement dates from the late 1840s.

Plate 18 The superb hanging stair of David Hamilton's No 6 Monteith Row (the front elevation of this building can be seen in Plate 50). This was the only example of a stair-tower containing a hanging stair known to the author.

Plate 19 (*top*) The kitchen of a Room-and-kitchen house, 1946. The overmantel is an unusual addition to kitchen fittings and would have looked less out of place in the Room.

Plate 20 (*above*) A single-end in Howard Street, now Finnart Street, Bridgeton (*c* 1907). This is City Improvement Trust housing of 1905 and well illustrates that a single-end was not necessarily a slum. For a single person, in fact, it was ideal.

time were commuted to monetary payments made twice yearly at the terms of Martinmas and Whitsunday. These feudal links produced a special phraseology in which the Crown was superior over all, under it being the king's vassals who, in their turn as subject superiors, had vassals who might again be subject superiors, and so on almost *ad infinitum*. Each superior, on *feuing* some of his land, granted a charter to his new vassal, who in return agreed to render certain services, or to pay, in money or in kind, what was known as *feu duty*.

Inside burghs a system arose whereby, instead of a superior selling his ground for an overall price, he converted it into an annual payment, secured on the value of the ground and appropriately called a *ground annual*. Similarly, outside the burgh boundary, it became common practice, when offering vacant ground for sale, to convert the price into a feu duty payable half-yearly. The feudal system had thus, by the time these changes were taking place in the nineteenth century, been brought up to date. At five per cent return on money, a purchase price of £100, for example, would produce a feu duty or ground annual of £5 *per annum*.

In the second half of the twentieth century, a movement was started in Scotland to abolish feu duty, on the grounds that it was an imposition for which no return was given (when on the contrary the feu duty in most cases was the conversion into an annual payment of the whole or part of the original price of the ground). In addition, such a fixed payment was something highly unusual in modern times, with the rapid depreciation of money. New feu duties were eventually abolished under the Land Tenure Reform (Scotland) Act of 1974, and provision was made for compulsory redemption in stages.

The influence of the feudal system on the development of the tenement can be seen from the use of the title-deeds to incorporate special clauses of control. When town-planning and estate management began in the mid-eighteenth century, we find that the superior used the land-grant system to write into the title-deeds a new set of clauses controlling the use of the land, and eventually the very size and style of the buildings which could be erected on it. The power to exercise this kind of control belonged to the superior alone until the twentieth century, when the many difficulties encountered in redeveloping ground for the second or third time made it necessary to place these controls in the hands of a central authority.

In Glasgow in the late eighteenth century, therefore, we find building developments controlled entirely by the superiors. These were chiefly landowners possessing farmland on the outskirts of the city, who began to consider the possibility of augmenting their income from the granting of building-feus, and they were quickly followed by the city fathers and the merchant and trade guilds.

In some instances, as the first step towards forming a new housing estate, the owner would lay down the streets preparatory to granting any of the building plots and, after the introduction of a public water supply, would also construct the sewer. The first clause in the title of a building plot would, therefore, often be an obligation on the feuar to form the street and sewer *ex adverso* (alongside) the feu, or to repay half the cost, if the work had already been done.[8]

If the landowner had any particular scheme in mind for the type and standard of the building, the next clause in the feu contract would lay down that a structure of that particular description must be erected. The building had also to be completed within a specified period. After all, in many cases the owner had not been paid for his ground — the price, as mentioned above, having been converted into an annual feu duty — and he naturally wanted a revenue-producing development on the ground as soon as possible to give him security for his feu duty. In districts intended for development as residential areas in which tenements were to be built, this clause would also specify the maximum number of stories and the minimum number of rooms to be provided in each house. The material to be used was specified — usually stone — with any special treatment of the street frontage, such as facing with polished ashlar, which became the norm in Glasgow in the nineteenth century. The roof was directed to be slated, and all woodwork to be of the best foreign timber.[9] Finally, the plans of the proposed building required to be passed by the superior before operations commenced, and it should be remembered that, outside burghs, there was no other authority to examine the plans for safety or amenity.

Among the earliest superiors in Glasgow to place prohibitive clauses in his title-deeds was Bailie John Shortridge. In 1761 he built a tenement, or 'Four-story Land' on the corner of Argyle Street and Dunlop Street and, with an apparently profound knowledge of the personal habits of the burghers of the old city, introduced a series of regulations to keep them under control. It was laid down that the occupants were

> Not to fix any Broads or Boxes without the Kitchen Windows, either for Throwing out of Water, or any Nestiness, or Dropping of Bottles, the Foul Water being to be Conveyed from the Kitchen in the said Tenement by a

Lead Pipe; no Nestiness or Water shall be thrown out at any of the Windows, nor shall Carpets or Floor cloaths be Shaken or Cleaned over any of the Fore-Windows looking to Argyle Street, but shall be Cleaned over the Pass-Windows, under the Penalty of Five Shillings for each Transgression. The Dung or Fulzie to be made in the Tenement is to be carried to the Middenstead belonging to the Land, and to be laid down thereon . . . [when it became the exclusive property of the Bailie who, on his part] . . . undertakes to keep the Midden decent, by Carrying away the Contents four times each year, or oftener, if needful.[10]

As another example of the conditions a superior could lay down in feu-contracts, those made by the City Improvement Trust for the regulation of their new estate at Overnewton in 1871 may be cited. Buildings there had to be of four square stories with no attics or sunk-stories. There were to be no shops or places of business of any kind except facing Old Dumbarton Road, where both shops and basements for storage were allowed. Houses were to have not less than two and not more than three apartments, except for those facing Old Dumbarton Road, which were to have not less than two and not more than four apartments. There were to be no back buildings other than wash-houses and ash-pits. The fronts of the tenements had to be of dressed and polished ashlar. In this way, decent conditions were assured before the days of buildings regulations.[11]

Owing to the wealth of coal and ironstone, a special clause in most feu contracts in the west of Scotland reserved to the superior the right to the minerals under any ground sold, with power to work them should he so wish. The right of compensation for damage to buildings on the surface was, however, granted to the vassal at the same time. A superior could not expect to make money out of both the minerals and the surface ground — he had to compromise!

The five simple rules already mentioned as forming the common law of the tenement sufficed in principle into the twentieth century, when title-deeds began to contain clauses which modified them in order to suit modern requirements. Such clauses provide that:

A   The whole plot of ground, the walls, roof, passages and stairs of the tenement are common property.

B   This common property is to be maintained by all the owners in some equitable proportion.

C   Various rules of administration are to be observed as approved by a quorum of the proprietors, such as the amount of common insurance, the standard of maintenance, etc.[12]

The twentieth-century builder who wants to sell his flats incorporates these, and any other conditions he wishes to enforce, into the feu contracts entered into with the individual flat owner, and thus makes them conditions of the feu.

Statutory Legislation

The rapid growth of many Scottish burghs in the nineteenth century made it necessary to add considerably to the existing controls examined in Part 1 of this chapter, by means of parliamentary legislation.

In 1800, the first Glasgow Police Act was passed.[13] It had an immediate and not altogether beneficial effect. For the first time, a rate on the assessed rental of all city property was imposed, graduating from 4d in the pound on annual rents between £4 and £6, to 1s on rents of £15 upwards. In a sense it was a reform Act also, for it gave the citizens some control over, and voice in, the election of their representatives.

This Act made obligatory the laying-down of foot pavements, under the eye of the Dean of Guild Court, and the daily sweeping, scraping or cleansing of the same, under pain of a fine of 1s for each offence! Clause 24 ordered the proprietors of all houses and other buildings fronting the streets of the city to remove all 'Outstairs, Outshots, Buildings, Erections, and Other Things whatsoever, which tend to obstruct free passage in the said streets and foot pavements.' The public streets themselves were to be cleansed and swept by publicly appointed scavengers, and common sewers formed to drain them. Clause 89 turned to the improvement of old properties, and remarked that

> the shops fronting some of the streets ... are situated in piazzas behind pillars, whereby the said shops are not only rendered dark and incommodious, but the said piazzas in the Evenings and at Night are receptacles for Thieves, Pickpockets, and idle and disorderly Persons ... [and powers were granted to the shopkeepers to bring forward their shops] ... to the front of the said Pillars, so as to include the Area of the said Piazzas into the shops.

The 1800 Act, designed to be in force for a limited period only, was replaced in 1807 by another which modified its provisions.[14] As might have been expected, the rates were increased to a new scale of 5d to 1s 3d 'in order to raise a Fund for defraying the Expense of the Establishment of a Master of Police, Superintendent of Fire Engines,

Collector, Treasurer, Clerks, Servants, Firemen, Watchmen, and other proper Officers ...'. Occupiers of dwelling houses, shops, warehouses or workshops where a fire broke out were to be fined the sum of £5 sterling to pay the wages of the firemen and the cost of extinguishing the blaze.

These first two acts were followed in 1821 by a third, which largely continued the same enactments.[15] One, however, was given a new corollary. Authorisation for the erection of public street-lamps was continued, but now the authorities were given leave 'to enter into Contracts for lighting such Lamps either by means of Oil, or with Lights known by the Name of Gas Lights'.

The next Act, passed in 1843, contained no fewer than 287 clauses.[16] The Dean of Guild Court now appears as a body with well-defined powers and enlarged authority over old and new buildings. Old buildings which could be considered 'insecure, ruinous, or in any other way dangerous to the safety of the inhabitants' could be ordered to be demolished. Building lines were established, and all new buildings compelled to adhere to them.

The regulations were also extended to cover the interior of buildings:

> The possessor of every house, flat or story, entered by a common stair, shall cause the stair and areas immediately below the flat or story possessed by him, to be swept every lawful day, and washed at least once a week ... under a penalty not exceeding 5 shillings for each offence.

Permission could be given to proprietors of tenements to construct a water-supply pipe and to connect it to the main pipe in the street. Similarly, waste-pipes could be connected to the common sewer, both of these operations to be supervised by the Dean of Guild.

The 1846 Police Act was notable for the far-reaching consequences it had in the administrative field.[17] Under it, the burghs of the Gorbals, Anderston and the Calton were absorbed into the new municipality of Glasgow. The earlier governing body under the previous Acts, the Board of Police Commissioners, was abolished, and its function taken over by a town council, elected by the citizens. This remained the constitutional arrangement until the 1970s.

Overcrowding and its consequent evils reached their height in the 1840s, and the new Town Council realised that drastic action was needed to remedy the situation. The sum of £30 000 was set aside to acquire the worst of the old properties in the city centre, but this proved to be totally inadequate. The lack of any building regulations or proper legislation to control the manner of building new houses, which has been mentioned in the first part of this chapter, was resulting in new districts springing up around the city which were as objectionable as the old. In order to exercise greater control, the 1862 General Police and Improvement Act (Scotland) was passed.[18]

This was the first Act to attempt control over hygiene and sanitary matters as well as over the buildings themselves. Section 210 dealt with water supply and sanitation thus:

> ... the owner of every House or Part of a House occupied by a separate family, into which Water has not been already introduced, shall introduce Water into every such House ... within the Burgh, by means of a Pipe not less than Half-an-inch Bore, fitted with a Crane opening upon the sink and soil-pipe after-mentioned, and shall fit up, in some Window, Recess, or other well-lighted and ventilated Place, a Sink, to be connected with a Soil-Pipe, duly trapped, leading into the nearest Drain, sufficient to carry off the whole Foul Water, and ... every such owner shall also provide for such House or Part of a House occupied by a separate family, wherever practicable, a sufficient water-closet.

The intentions of the Act were wholly admirable and resulted in an adequate internal water supply to the great majority of houses. However, the qualification 'wherever practicable', in relation to the provision of water-closets, allowed many proprietors to ignore that part of the clause altogether.

The first water supply in Glasgow had been provided by the Glasgow Water Works Company, a body set up by Act of Parliament in 1806.[19] The water was taken from the River Clyde and collected in reservoirs in the east end of the city before being piped through the streets. In 1808 a rival company was set up in the west end, called the Cranstonhill Water Works Company, which also utilised water pumped from the river.[20] It was not so successful as its rival, despite obtaining further powers from Parliament, and the two companies eventually amalgamated in 1838.

The earliest record of the water supply existing dates from the year of the union of the two companies and shows that in that year six and a half million gallons were supplied daily to a population of 250 000 — an average of twenty-six gallons per head.[21] The quality of the water, never very good, deteriorated with the passing of time, owing to the lack of effective filtering plant. As a result, a number of schemes were devised for an alternative supply during the 1840s. The only one of these to be carried out was that of the Gorbals Gravitation Water Company, which received Parliamentary assent in 1846 and which was planned to supply just that limited area of the city. The quality of the water provided by this company was much superior, being brought from the hills some miles south of the city, and the reservoirs were twice extended to cover a wider area of supply.[22]

Despite the success of the Gorbals works, however, the supply of good water to the rest of the city was quite inadequate, and in 1855 an Act of Parliament was obtained to bring water from Loch Katrine.[23] This scheme, astonishingly ambitious and far-sighted as it was for the mid-nineteenth century, was inaugurated by Queen Victoria on 21 July 1859 and has ever since been a source of pride to the city.[24] It made it possible for the 1862 Police Act to decree that water must be introduced into every house in the city.

The attempts by the Town Council to remove the worst of the over-crowded and dilapidated buildings had been woefully inadequate, and the problem was tackled again in 1866 with the creation of the City Improvement Trust. The Act which brought it into being opens with a preamble:

> Various Portions of the City of Glasgow are so built, and the Buildings thereon are so densely inhabited as to be highly injurious to the moral and physical welfare of the Inhabitants, and many of the Thoroughfares are narrow, circuitous, and inconvenient. . . . it would be of public and local Advantage if various Houses and Buildings were taken down, and those portions of the said City reconstituted, and new streets were constructed in and through various Parts of the said City.[25]

Under the provisions of this Act, the Town Council were empowered to acquire old properties, by compulsory purchase, within an overall area of eighty-eight acres, to demolish them and, after realigning the streets, to control the rebuilding, thus preventing a recurrence of the overcrowding and piecemeal building which had been in vogue before. In addition, they had power to acquire land for the purpose of rehousing the ejected tenants, and also to erect model lodging-houses for the accommodation of the very poorest class.

Meanwhile, the first general Public Health (Scotland) Act of 1867 reinforced some of the clauses of 1862 by providing 'that in the event of any insufficiency of light, defect of structure, defect of ventilation, want of repair or proper drainage, or suitable water-closet or privy accommodation' the Sheriff was empowered to prohibit a building from being used as a dwelling-house.[26]

In 1878, Glasgow Town Council petitioned the Home Secretary, submitting to him a provisional order containing amendments to the 1866 Act. A public enquiry was held in February 1879 into the proposed amendments, which in fact formed a series of building regulations. Among the proposals was one which would disallow the four corner-tenements of a square in order to allow a free passage of air to circulate in the back-courts, which themselves were to be greatly increased in size. Among a variety of new internal regulations, the ceiling height was to be not less than 10 feet. Needless to say, there were many objectors to the scheme, notably the Glasgow Institute of Architects, the Faculty of Procurators and a number of city landlords and factors, who stood to lose considerably, were the new proposals put into effect. Their arguments finally won the day, and the proposals were abandoned for the time being.

'An Act for regulating the Police and Sanitary Administration of towns and populous places, and for facilitating the union of Police and Municipal Administration in Burghs in Scotland.' Such is the full title of the Burgh Police (Scotland) Act of 1892.[27] It had 518 clauses, and was more comprehensive and influential than any of its predecessors. One clause deals in detail with the obligation on tenement dwellers to keep the common stair and landings clean. Others deal with the erection of new buildings, and contain a set of detailed regulations. To quote one example:

> No new tenement of houses, except ... in special circumstances ... shall have more than 12 dwelling houses entering from one common stair or passage, where the common stair or passage is within the tenement, but where there is an outside stair with balconies, 24 houses may be permitted.

The width of stairs and passages was to be not less than 4 feet. Every habitable room on the ground floor was to be at least 9 ft 6 in, and on other floors at least 9 feet in height from floor to ceiling, with attics at least 8 feet in height. In addition, every habitable room was to have a window with a total glazed area of at least one tenth of the area of the room.

These regulations were considerably amplified in a later document, the Glasgow Building Regulations Act of 1900.[28] Among many new details regarding dwelling-houses were the following:

No dwelling-house shall hereafter be provided or constructed in any new or existing building which shall exclusive of any lobbies, closets, presses, and recesses therein, be less than

Dwelling houses of 1 apartment   1000 cu ft
Dwelling houses of 2 apartments   1600 cu ft
Dwelling houses of 3 apartments   2400 cu ft

No dwelling house shall contain an enclosed bed or a bed recess which is not open in front for three quarters of its length, and from floor to ceiling. .... This provision shall, after the expiry of 5 years from the passing of this Act apply to existing dwelling houses.

The thickness of external walls was also prescribed, for this was the age when a new building material, concrete, was coming into use.

Following on the provisions of this Act, Glasgow Corporation drew up a series of detailed by-laws strictly controlling new buildings and constructional methods, and these form the basis of present day legislation on these matters. They are contained in the Building Standards (Scotland) Regulations, which first appeared in 1953, and have been regularly revised since in the light of changing conditions. This being an age of multi-story flats and a multiplicity of electric fitments, regulations have naturally been brought in to control them. The latest improvement (1972) has been the conversion of all measurements to those of the metric scale, in a way reviving the ancient Scottish links with the continent of Europe.[29] Legislation affecting building and finance during the twentieth century will be found in the appropriate places in Chapters 9, 10 and 11.

1 *30 & 31 Vict c 101*, the Public Health (Scotland) Act 1867. J Skelton, *Skelton's Handbook of Public Health* (ed J P Macdougall and A Murray 1898) p 18.
2 J D Marwick (ed), *Charters and Other Documents Relating to the City of Glasgow* (3 vols, 1897–1906), *1649–1707* p 574, where there is an example of this right in the form of an agreement between two proprietors in the Trongate:

> Mr Hew [Eglintoun] grantis licens to the said William to draw the paittis of his gavill, rais and big the same to sic heicht as he pleissis, and to raggall his sclait ruif thairintill, provyding the said William mak the twa chymnayis in his said gavill sufficientlie raisit and buskit abone with sufficient work and paittit according as thai ar presentlie situat for passage of the reik, and to mak his tenement in als gud estait in thak and rigging as the said William sall demoleis the samyn ...

3 Marwick, *Charters and Other Documents, 1175–1649* p 3.
4 *ibid, 1175–1649* p 28. *Blench farm* was a feudal contract with a nominal feu duty which was paid only on demand.

5 Bell and Paton, p 11.
6 Gordon, *Glasghu facies* vol 1 p 361. For example, Edinburgh, Peebles and Stirling. While the existence of city walls around Glasgow may be disputed, it is quite certain that there was a ditch in certain parts, presumably to mark the boundary between natural watercourses.
7 See Marwick, *Charters and Other Documents, 1175–1649* p dcxxv, where a detailed list may be found.
8 Cleland, *Abridgment of the Annals* p 475, details forty-three sewers in the city streets formed prior to May 1817.
9 The Calton Burgh Police Act 1819, p 10. 'Proprietors are hereby prohibited from thatching with straw, Broom, Heath, Rushes, Reeds, or Fern, and from covering with Tar, Pitch, or Paper the roofs of [new and rebuilt] tenements.' The idea of a building with a paper roof is fascinating!
10 Gordon, *Glasghu facies* vol 2, p 1026.
11 *Minutes of the Glasgow City Improvement Trust,* 10 January 1871.
12 I Connell, *Law affecting Building Operations and Architects' and Builders' Contracts* (1903). Chapter on the Law of the Tenement, p 103.
13 *39 & 40 Geo III c 88* (1800) 'An Act for extending the Royalty of the City of Glasgow over certain adjacent lands; for paving, lighting and cleansing the Streets, for regulating the Police, and appointing Officers and Watchmen; for dividing the city into Wards, and appointing Commissioners etc.'
14 *47 Geo III c 29.*
15 *1 & 2 Geo IV c 48.*
16 *6 & 7 Vict c 99.*
17 9 & 10 Vict c 289.
18 *25 & 26 Vict c 101.*
19 *46 Geo III c 136.* 'An Act for supplying the City and Suburbs with Water.'
20 *48 Geo III c 44.* 'An Act for the further Supply of the City and Suburbs of Glasgow and Places adjacent with Water.'
21 J Burnet, *History of the Water Supply of Glasgow* (1869) gives a very full account of the subject on p 16.
22 *9 & 10 Vict c 347.* The Gorbals Gravitation Water Company Act 1846. The amendment Acts of 1850 and 1853 extended the water supply to Renfrew, Barrhead, Nitshill and Rutherglen (*13 & 14 Vict c 92* and *16 & 17 Vict c 98*). For a full account, see Burnet.
23 *18 & 19 Vict c 118.*
24 Much information on this scheme will be found in both Burnet, and J D Marwick, *Glasgow — the Water Supply of the City* (1901).
25 *29 Vict c 85.*
26 *30 & 31 Vict c 101.*
27 *55 & 56 Vict c 55.*
28 *63 & 64 Vict c 150.*
29 The Building Standards (Scotland) (Consolidation) Regulations 1971.

ARCHITECTURE

3
The Exterior

The following two chapters describe characteristic features of tenement design and explore their evolution during the nineteenth century. The layout and facilities of typical tenement houses are also studied. Descriptions are confined to buildings erected during the nineteenth century because this is the period which might well be described as the 'Golden Age' of the tenement, when the greatest variety and invention was possible.

It is the street elevation of the tenement which impresses itself on the visitor to the city (Plate 8). The long vistas of anonymous stone frontages, stretching in apparently endless lines, form what has long been accepted as the typical street backcloth. Glasgow, luckily, has the advantage of being built upon a number of hills, and this effectively prevents the monotony which a level site would have produced. The solid, dignified stone frontages are typical of the best tradition of Scottish building, and have always come as something of a surprise to visitors used to a different style and materials.

In attempting to evaluate these street frontages, it must be borne in mind that in relatively few cases was an entire range erected by a single builder. As already noted, districts were usually developed piecemeal by a number of builders, each building on two or three steadings at a time, without too much thought as to the architectural unity of the whole scheme. That was entirely dependent upon the superior, as explained in Chapter 2. However, by the early nineteenth century a tradition of elevational design had become established, which meant that adjacent tenements, although erected by different builders, tended to be very similar in appearance. In addition, being built with mutual gables meant that each tenement merged with its neighbours, only the close entrance giving a clue to individual identity. This apparently continuously-designed frontage enabled some of the more ingenious architects to link their plans to form double or even triple tenements which are impossible to distinguish from external appearance alone.

In the early nineteenth century, when architecture was becoming more and more retrospective, it was natural that designers should turn to earlier European architectural achievement for inspiration. The origin of many tenement elevations is to be found in the Renaissance palaces of Rome and northern Italy. Two Roman examples may be considered. The Palazzo della Cancelleria, one of the earliest important Renaissance buildings in that city, is substantially a three-storied structure with a long frontage of fourteen bays (Plate 9). The ground floor treatment is simple, with small arched windows set in a heavily rusticated wall. This somewhat defensive appearance conceals the main storage space. The first floor, containing the public apartments, is the most elaborately treated, having arched windows contained within a moulded surround with entablature. The rhythm of the window openings is further emphasised by the use of Corinthian pilasters between the bays. The second floor is somewhat similar, but with smaller openings.

The Palazzo Pietro Massimi is unusual in having a curved frontage and containing four stories. The ground floor has pilasters and is of greater height than those above, an idea readily transferable to a tenement containing shops on the ground floor. The first floor has large windows with entablature and consoles — a design adopted in hundreds of Glasgow tenements. The smaller windows of the two upper floors also find their counterpart in Glasgow, for the Scottish architects frequently played down this section of their elevations.

Both these examples have a distinct horizontal emphasis, which in the Cancelleria Palace is further underlined by moulded string-courses and cornices across the full width of the building. Such features may also be frequently found in Glasgow. Alternatively, but more rarely, a vertical emphasis was thought desirable, and this was achieved by linking two stories by pilasters or recesses.

In Glasgow, better-class tenements never contained shops, but working-class examples were frequently designed with an interchangeable ground floor — a two-apartment house being readily convertible into a shop with back room, or vice versa. Where shops only were envisaged, for example along the main thoroughfares, the ground-floor ceiling is abnormally high, to allow for storage space and adequate ventilation. As might be expected, few original shopfronts with their cast-iron columns remain, the dictates of fashion having long ago demanded their replacement.

The main apartments of the Renaissance palace were always on the first floor — the *piano nobile* — and the idea of emphasising this flat persisted beyond the adaptation of the style for multiple occupation. Not only was the front elevation of this floor more elaborately treated, with moulded surround, entablature, consoles and sometimes pediments, but internally the ceiling height was often greater. One floor up was considered ideal — away from the noise, smell and dirt of the street, yet not too far to climb. The first-floor house was comfortable too, kept warm by the story beneath and not losing heat through a roof above.

The second floor, only less desirable in that there were more stairs to climb, usually had slightly less elaborate treatment externally, with surround and entablature only. The third floor, where there was one, was usually left plain, although some architects, like Alexander 'Greek' Thomson, singled it out for special treatment.

The value of window openings as a unifying feature of elevational design is obvious and was very seriously considered by architects, particularly in the first half of the century. In order to achieve an unbroken rhythm, they frequently employed the device of *blind windows* which, on occasion, could be glazed to heighten the illusion.[1] These blind windows had nothing to do with the window-tax. On examination, one will usually find that behind them is a fireplace or a cupboard, so that no real window could ever have been in that position.

In the second half of the century, windows began to grow larger. Instead of single lights divided into two sashes, each containing six small panes, two and three lights became common, often fitted with larger panes of plate glass when that material became cheaper. The first building in Glasgow to be entirely glazed with plate glass was erected in 1852,[2] and the new material rapidly became popular. Another important change in window design was the extension of the parlour window into a bow or oriel, sometimes semi-circular but more often three-sided. This innovation appeared as early as the 1840s, but did not become general until forty years later.[3]

Doorways take a number of different forms. In working-class tenements, the entrance to the *close*, or passage leading to the stair, was generally simply a rectangular opening in the wall surface. In better-class examples, it might have an entablature and consoles to match the windows on the floor above. Where the ground-floor houses had separate entrances, these too were often elaborately treated. In Abbotsford Place, for example, they had projecting porches, with Corinthian or Ionic columns supporting an entablature, with the doorway itself enclosed within a coved recess. (See Fig 5, on p 80) Other examples made an even more prominent feature of these doorways by giving them square pillared porches reached by a flight of steps from street level. This treatment is perhaps best seen at Breadalbane Terrace in Hill Street, Garnethill, where the porches, regularly placed at the entrances to both closes and main-door houses, effectively break up the elevation. Porches of similar type but without the steps are found at St Vincent Crescent.

Examination of the varying treatment of the ground plan of the tenement reveals an evolutionary process throughout the first half of the century. This process is best studied by co-relating the ground-floor access and the common stair. An early type of tenement was a simple two-storied building, the ground-floor houses of which entered directly from the street, while the upper floor was reached by a projecting open stair at the back. Access to this stair was by means of an open passage at one side of the tenement. This particular type of building became common throughout the industrial midlands of Scotland, and was still being erected up to World War I.

Owing to the rapid increase of population in the larger towns, the two stories of such tenements were soon increased to three, for which the staircase, now circular in form, was enclosed within a tower. A development of this idea had a passage through the building from the street to the back-court. At first this was not aligned with the stair, and it was necessary to go out into the open air again before entering the stair-tower. In middle-class Laurieston in particular, an important variation of this occurred, involving double tenements with a central close and two stair-towers (Plate 11).

The circular or *turnpike* stair rose from bottom to top almost continuously, with only a tiny landing on each floor. It almost always had a central stone newel, although examples existed of open-centred, or *hanging* stairs (Plate 18).

Having achieved a link between the close and stair, the next consideration was the doubtful advantage of having the common stair outside the walls of the main building. In Georgian Glasgow, when builders wanted to utilise every square foot of available space for domestic use, it was a distinct advantage to place the stair outside, enabling the whole area within the walls to be occupied by one or two houses. On the other hand, this advantage was nullified in poorer-class tenements, because a passage had to be inserted to allow access to the greater number of small houses.

Intermediate stages occur when the circular stair was brought first half, and then two-thirds within the building, and eventually it appears entirely within the walls, being lit by windows in the back wall.

By the middle of the century the circular stair was being replaced in popularity by the rectangular type in two parallel flights of nine or ten steps each from landing to landing. In early examples there was a narrow open well, sometimes only an inch or two wide, but by mid-century the centre had become a solid wall screening each flight from the next, strengthening the stair, and also preventing accidents. It was this latter type which became normal after about 1880 and has continued so ever since. Sometimes the placing of close and stair was reversed, with the latter rising at the front of the building — a plan much favoured in Edinburgh, but also found in certain districts of Glasgow.[4]

An earlier form continued contemporaneously with the evolution of the back stair. This was the central stair, for the design of which Robert Adam has been given the credit. It was generally more spacious than the back-stair, with an open well in the centre to allow the light to reach the foot. In the earliest examples it was circular or elliptical in plan, but later usually rectangular, with the stair rising in two flights. Efficient lighting was a problem. It had to be lit from above — from a cupola or skylight in the roof — and this meant almost inevitably a dark stair-foot.[5] The 1892 Glasgow Building Regulations Act tackled this problem by laying down the size of the stair-well, which had to be 18, 23 or 30 square feet, when the height of the tenement was two, three or four stories respectively. The skylight had to have a superficial area equal to five times that of the well-hole of the stair, and finally, the staircase itself had to be not less than 3 ft 9 in wide. Eventually, because of the difficulty of lighting and ventilating it adequately, the central-stair plan fell from favour except in corner-tenements where no back-lighting was possible.

Without any doubt, the rectangular *dogleg* or *scale-and-platt* stair against the back wall was by far the best arrangement, allowing as it did adequate ventilation and light for the total height of the building. The size of the stair window gradually increased towards the end of the century, and from the 1890s stair-windows were often filled with painted glass in a variety of Art Nouveau designs, as may be seen in

31

Hyndland or Langside.

In working-class areas, vehicular access was often required through a tenement to a factory or workshop situated in the hollow square behind, and this was provided by means of a *pend*, or cart-entrance. In order not to waste further space, architects often designed their stairs to enter from one side of the pend.

The close has always been a significant feature of Glasgow social life, a place of continuous activity: sweeping, washing, meeting one's neighbours, sheltering from a sudden shower. In many respects, it is really an extension of the street, and this idea is heightened in Glasgow, where the street entrance is traditionally open.[6] This presents a very different picture from Edinburgh, where every close still has its door and set of polished bell-knobs, each landing having a manually-operated mechanism by which the door may be opened — a very much more private way of life. However, West Prince's Street and St Vincent Crescent are two Glasgow areas where this system was employed.[7] It is also now customary in reconstructed tenements to have a door at the street entrance to the close.

A minimum width of 4 feet was laid down for closes by the 1866 Police Act, irrespective of the number of houses or back-lands the close led to. Although the adequacy of this width was questioned in 1878, when the corporation endeavoured to have it extended to 5 feet, the idea was not approved, mainly because the number of back-lands was growing fewer and 4 feet was considered by most authorities to be perfectly adequate for a single building.[8] The close was paved with durable Caithness slabs, easily kept clean by the weekly washing, and usually had a door-scraper at the entrance, set in a small recess. High-class tenements, for example those on Garnethill, boasted a pair of grand cast-iron scrapers on the top step, outside the door.

The close walls were plastered and whitewashed, and often had the odd feature of a number of flues carried diagonally across the ceiling. In better-class tenements the lower part of the close-wall was painted, often with a stencilled pattern above. Eventually, in the 1890s, this was replaced by an easily-cleaned tiled dado, about 5 ft 3 in in height — creating the so-called 'wally close', which was a source of inordinate pride to those privileged to dwell in it. The very best tenements had tiles up the staircase also (Plate 13).

If the back-court was on a lower level than the street, the stair continued down to the basement, the dark and unattractive area at the foot being known locally as 'the dunny'. The basements sometimes contained houses but more frequently were occupied by the wash-house and cellars for the dwellers above. A wooden door usually secured the back-court.

When the more socially conscious proprietors began to provide internal sanitary accommodation for their tenants, a communal wc was usually fitted off one side of the half- or mid-landing of the stair for the use of those on the floor above. Sometimes this small chamber partly projected into the flat above, forming a curious and useless raised area in one corner of the kitchen.

The back elevation of a tenement is quite different from the front. The windows are less regularly spaced and of different sizes, with the stair window at a different level from the rest. The stonework is generally inferior, being coursed rubble and not the polished ashlar of the street front. In the early nineteenth century both were of the local freestone which, although technically referred to as 'white', was in reality an attractive honey-colour and came from a number of quarries around the city, such as Kenmure, Westfield or Giffnock. By 1890 the quality of the stone from these quarries had deteriorated so badly that it became necessary to seek supplies elsewhere. These were found near Lockerbie, near Dumfries and at Ballochmyle in south Ayrshire, and were transported to the city by rail. As this new stone was red in colour, it made a big difference to the appearance of the new buildings put up from that time. The local white stone, however, continued to be used for back walls and sometimes for gables.

Brick was not used much externally before the 1870s, when gables and back walls began to be built of this material, particularly in the east end at Bridgeton and Parkhead, which were in the neighbourhood of many brickworks on the eastern clayfield. Previously its use had been largely confined to internal walling. This may have been caused by the imposition of a tax on bricks which began in 1784 at the rate of 2s 6d per thousand and which rose to 5s 10d in 1839. This tax was always considered to be an obstacle to the improvement of working-class housing but, despite repeated protests from the building trade, was not abolished until 1850.

The circular stair-towers formed the dominating feature of the back elevations of countless early nineteenth-century tenements. Today they are hard to find. Usually of red brick, although some were certainly of stone, they rise to four stories, or four stories and attic in height.[9] It may seem strange to find a brick stair-tower attached to a stone tenement, and it can only be explained by the fact that it is easier to build a circular structure in brick than in stone. One can see how common they were at one time by looking at the early editions of the Ordnance Survey maps of the city. The finest example was the east side of Abbotsford Place which boasted no fewer than sixteen towers serving its eight double tenements (Plate 14). Its unnecessary demolition a few years ago was a major loss to Scottish architecture.

Not to be confused with the stair-tower is the wc stack, which is a smaller structure also affixed to the back wall. It generally consists of a small rectangular four-story tower, usually of brick, housing a single wc for communal use on each half-landing. The tenements around Gorbals Cross, built in the 1870s, were provided with a small cast-iron closet housed in a narrow stack. The great majority of these stacks date from the period following the passing of the 1892 Police Act, which made internal sanitation compulsory, and they replaced the primitive dry-closet, or privy, in the back-court, which had previously served the whole tenement. In many cases, the necessary alterations included the formation of a new landing within the extension as well as the closet itself. Impecunious proprietors, needless to say, provided only the smallest possible addition which could obtain the sanction of the Dean of Guild Court. Where the wc stack is contemporary with the tenement, it is almost always of stone and triangular in shape to allow for a small landing.

There were some variations on this theme. The tenements erected by Glasgow Corporation, whether in their capacity as Police Commissioners or as Trustees under the City Improvement Act, provided from the 1870s the luxury of two wcs on each landing — one for each sex![10] In the tenements erected in connection with the fire station in Nicholson Street, there was an exceptionally spacious open landing with an iron railing, and a tiny closet of cast-iron somewhat precariously perched on each side (Plate 16).

The back-court, or drying-green, was the common property of everyone living in the tenement. It sometimes contained a communal wash-house, if this was not fitted into the basement, and this, with its cast-iron boiler heated by means of a coal fire beneath, was available to all the residents on a rota basis. Needless to say this system could lead to strained relationships among the tenants. One could not change one's wash-day to suit circumstances, and the whereabouts of that indispensable item, the wash-house key, was a frequent source of friction. The green was provided with iron clothes-poles and here, usually ranged along one side, were the ash-pits, replacing the dungstead and privies of earlier generations. Perhaps nothing illustrates changing conditions more than these. In the seventeenth and eighteenth centuries the contents were sold as manure, and formed a valuable source of income to the proprietor, whereas by the second half of the nineteenth century the whole operation had become a necessary but irksome duty.

This back-court is the original *Closs* or *Close* — an enclosed space — the term only changing its meaning during the nineteenth century to refer to the common passage from the street to the back-court. In 1800, a typical advertisement appears in the *Glasgow Courier*, in which 'Each lodging will have . . . the privilege of a Well in the back closs.' [11] This private well would later be provided with a pump, and later still, when piped water was introduced, a tap enclosed in a wooden box would be available, each resident having a key. As has already been noticed in Chapter 2, the 1862 Police Act compelled all landlords to bring a piped water supply inside the building where this had not been already done. The result was many curious arrangements whereby sinks were placed outside stair or kitchen windows with, as can be seen in old photographs, a timber canopy over them, to shelter the housewife during her time at the jawbox.

In the later years of the nineteenth century, tenements in the main streets of the city had a continuous row of shops on their ground floor. These were provided very often with projecting saloons or stores which occupied the limited area of the back-court. In such cases, the saloon's flat roof was used as the drying area, with the wash-house and ash-pits at first-floor level.

Another change in the appearance of the back of working-class tenements was the use of balconies as a means of access to the individual houses on each floor. According to the provisions of the 1892 Police Act, a tenement constructed in this way could contain twenty-four houses as opposed to twelve when the traditional internal stair and landings were used. Builders of single- and two-apartment houses were not slow to take advantage of this provision, which allowed so much more accommodation, and concrete balconies with their iron railings began to appear in many of the poorer areas. Details of tenements of this type erected by the City Improvement Trust and the Glasgow Workmen's Dwellings Company will be found in Chapter 9. It will be seen that this was in a sense a return to an earlier system — with a projecting stair-tower and galleries — which had been common in the late sixteenth and early seventeenth centuries.

The traditional tenement had a pitched roof covered with slates, and stone chimney-heads rising above the gables, sometimes in massive stacks enclosing as many as sixteen flues. In addition, smaller chimney-heads rose from the back or front walls as necessity demanded. Chimney-cans seem to have been in use from the second half of the eighteenth century. In 1806, the *Glasgow Herald* reported: 'Yesterday it blew a tremendous storm from the south-west, occasionally accompanied with heavy rain. A number of chimney tops and cans were blown down, by which several persons were hurt.'[12] The Dean of Guild promptly ordered all proprietors of houses within the city to have their chimney-stacks and cans examined, and repaired where necessary.[13]

Flat roofs were frowned upon until the 1890s, when lack of space for a back-court in congested districts left no alternative but to provide the wash-house and drying area on the asphalted roof. Even from that date only a limited number were allowed, such as the Improvement Trust's property at the top of Hope Street (where a school playground prevented a back-court), certain corner-buildings and a range in Pollokshaws Road at Crossmyloof. This last faced the Queen's Park and therefore five stories were allowed. A flat roof was necessary because a factory occupied the back space. The architect took extra care over this block of three tenements, making them quite fireproof.[14] This idea of a flat roof has been carried to its logical conclusion in the modern multi-story blocks where the roof-space as well as certain other areas on different floors have been set apart for laundry purposes.

1 Examples of glazed blind windows may be seen at Peel Terrace, Hill Street, at Walmer Crescent, Paisley Road West and occasionally elsewhere.
2 Bothwell Buildings, 2–28 Bothwell Street.
3 Bow windows are found at the back of the earlier section of Breadalbane Terrace, Hill Street, dating from 1845. Their first appearance on the front of a tenement is at La Belle Place in 1856.
4 Royal Crescent, 44–74 Queen's Drive, Crosshill, built in 1870, is an interesting example of a complete range of tenements (six in number) each of which has an open stair rising at the front of the building.
5 Large skylights of a purely functional kind were the commonest form of roof lighting. A particularly fine example of a circular cupola lighting a handsomely-proportioned stair can be seen at 148 Queen's Drive, Queen's Park.
6 Glasgow Provisional Order 1879 *Building Regulations Proceedings before Sheriff Clark* (1879). Evidence by Alexander Stewart, house factor, p 251.
7 Close doors were more common in middle-class developments outside the city limits. They can be found, for example, in all the tenements along Queen's Drive, Queen's Park and Stanmore Road, Mount Florida. All, however, were not provided with the mechanism on each landing to open the door.
8 Robert McCord, a builder giving evidence to the enquiry, thought 4 ft 6 in quite sufficient (*Building Regulations Proceedings*, p 208). John Honeyman, the architect, agreed with him (*ibid*, p 237).
9 A circular stone stair-tower still exists at 52 Virginia Street.
10 For example, in the Improvement Trust's own first block of tenements at the corner of the Saltmarket and Steel Street.
11 Advertisement in the *Glasgow Courier*, 28 January 1800.
12 *Glasgow Herald*, 26 December 1806.
13 *ibid*, 29 December 1806.

14 990–1004 Pollokshaws Road. The architect was John Nisbet, and they were erected in 1905–6 for John A Mactaggart. Springhill Gardens, close by, is another example (of a year earlier) by the same architect and builder.

4
The Interior

One of the greatest virtues of the tenement as a building-type is its adaptability. Depending on various circumstances, an ingenious architect could provide a remarkable variety of different house sizes and plans within the same solid, rectangular framework. The four-story Victorian tenement could contain five large houses of six or more apartments, or on a building-plot of the same size, to meet totally different requirements, twenty-five single-apartment houses. For the purposes of this chapter, which will deal with house interiors, an example of a large house from the early part of the century will be examined, followed by two typical working-class dwellings from the latter part — the *Room-and-kitchen*, and the *single-end*.

The first example is of a five-apartment house, containing dining-room, drawing-room, two bedrooms, kitchen, wc and lobby, typical of many erected in the 1830s or 1840s in Monteith Row, Abbotsford Place or Garnethill.

Entrance to the house was by a large, heavy, wide door, with its surface divided into panels by thin incised lines and with a brightly polished brass knob. To one side was a brass bell-pull, which rang a bell just inside the door at ceiling height. Above the door was a fanlight, sometimes with a delicate Adamesque design formed in ironwork. Frequently, however, it was divided into a number of rectangles with wooden astragals. The whole doorway was enclosed within a moulded surround. In the early house, the door would open directly into the lobby, no matter how big the house was. By the 1870s, however, it became customary in larger houses to provide a storm or outer door in two leaves, with a small vestibule and an inner door with a large pane of ornamental glass.

Of all the parts of a tenement flat, the *lobby* (*anglice*: hall) is the most variable in size and shape.[1] In the house here considered it would probably be roughly in the form of a large rectangle with most of the apartments leading directly from it. In area it would often be larger than a bedroom, and in some cases equal to the drawing-room in size. In addition to the doors to the various rooms there would be a *press*, or narrow cupboard, and a much larger storage-closet. Some of the internal doors would have fanlights, but even allowing for the borrowed light thus obtained, the lobby was never really well-lit unless all the doors were left open. From the centre of the ceiling hung a gas pendant with a single lamp, while the meter was usually on a shelf behind the outer door. All the better-class houses of this period would have had gas, as an Act of Parliament had been obtained in 1817 for building the city's first gasworks.[2] The lobby floor was invariably covered with oilcloth or linoleum, providing a surface which was hard-wearing and easily kept clean. A hatstand, a table and possibly an eight-day clock were the only articles of furniture.

The dining-room was often the largest apartment in the house. It usually had two windows to the front of the building, and one or sometimes two presses beside, or flanking, the fireplace. This latter was in the centre of the gable-wall, and had a large marble chimneypiece in simple Classical form with Doric pilasters and a moulded shelf. The marble, either black or white, was imported and carved in the marbleworks of one of the well-known firms which specialised in that kind of work. J and W Cleland and David Hamilton & Son were perhaps the best-known of these, the latter being run in conjunction with the architect's office at the top of Buchanan Street. Although the fireplace was provided by the proprietor, the grate was not and, on moving house, the nineteenth-century family took their grates with them. The dining room had what was called a *register grate* — in other words, one provided with a device for regulating the draught flow — with fender and fire-irons to match.
   Opposite the windows was a large store-closet, in which would be kept all the paraphernalia of the room which was not in immediate

39

use. Although similar in appearance and dimensions, this should not be confused with the *bed-closet* which is found in an identical position in smaller houses. The ceiling was generally eleven or twelve feet in height and had an ornamental plaster cornice, usually of Classical form, with egg-and-dart or leaf-and-dart mouldings. Sometimes, in addition, there was a continuous panel of vine leaves and fruit. In the middle was a large floral centrepiece from which a gasalier was suspended. This might consist of two or three branches and would be made of brass.

The wooden floor would be stained and polished, with a carpet covering the major portion. To obtain an idea of the furnishings of a typical dining-room, we cannot do better than quote two contemporary advertisements:

> A large and elegant Sideboard; a large and beautiful Set of Dining Tables; a set of Knives, cases filled; Breakfast Table; Window Curtains, Grate, Fire Irons and Fender, Dining-Room Chairs: Carpet and Rug, and a full set of Table China, with Glasses, Bottles, etc etc.[3]

That inventory was from a first-floor flat in Jamaica Street in 1806. The second is from a house in Steven Street, St George's Cross, and dates from 1865.

> Mahogany Dining Table, Rosewood Loo Table, 7 Mahogany Hair seated Chairs, Damask Curtains and Pole, Carpet and Rug, Two-light Gasalier, Register Grate, Fender, and Fire Irons.[4]

The size of rooms, of course, varied from house to house; the dining-room in the College Buildings in the High Street of 1793 measured roughly 21 feet by 16 feet, while a similar room of the 1860s, in New City Road, measured 19 feet by 15 feet. Drawing-rooms tended to be a little smaller. In the College Buildings they were roughly 18 feet by 15 feet, while in New City Road they were of the same size as the dining-rooms.[5]

The drawing-room or parlour had very similar arrangements to those already noted in the dining-room — two windows with curtains, venetian blinds and wooden shutters which folded back in double leaves into the wall on each side, a marble chimneypiece and a press. The ceiling was also ornamented, with a central roundel and hanging gas lamps. As this was primarily a sitting-room for leisure hours, there was not the same need for storage space. The Jamaica Street house contained the following:

> An elegant Set of Chairs, with two Sophas, Clips, etc;
> Window Curtains with Cornices; a pair of beautiful Tea
> Tables; Wilton Carpet; a Set of Tea and Coffee China,
> with two Plated Vases; Grate, Fire Irons, Fender, etc.

and the one in Steven Street, sixty years later:

> Rosewood Loo Table on Pillar and Claw; 6 Rosewood
> Chairs and Couch in Damask, Damask Window Curtains
> and Gilt Pole, Rosewood Cottage Pianoforte by Migeon, 7
> Octaves; Brussels Carpet and Rug, Two light Gasalier,
> Register Grate, Fender and Fire Irons etc.

Needless to say there was more variety in furnishing than these lists would seem to imply. An inventory of 1836 contained the following:

> Ladies' Work Table, with Chess Board, folding top
> etc: a few framed Engravings, a full length Duke of
> Wellington . . . [6]

and another from the same year:

> . . . an excellent Piano Forte, and several Oil Paintings with
> Superb Frames, and a Starling Bird in a Cage. [7]

As can be seen from the above lists, the drawing-room could have a variety of interesting furnishings! Loo tables (folding games-tables) were popular, as were tea-tables of different shapes and sizes. In the eighteenth century, a spinet was often found, replaced in the following century by the pianoforte — an instrument which grew in popularity as the Victorian era progressed, becoming the centrepiece of the musical evenings which were so much a feature of family entertainment at that time.

The bedrooms were smaller than either the dining- or drawing-rooms, and usually faced the back of the tenement. The arrangements in many cases were rather clumsy, as both window and fireplace had often to be fitted into the outside wall. The result was a small fireplace uncomfortably squeezed close against the corner of the room diagonally opposite the door. The ceiling was plain, with a single cornice-moulding. The fireplace contained the usual register grate with fire-irons and fender. There were considerably fewer articles of furniture than in the other apartments. In 1806, the bedrooms in the Jamaica Street houses were reported as having the following:

> Two full-mounted Bedsteads; three Feather Beds,

Mattresses and Blankets; two Chests of Drawers; Dressing Glasses; ditto Tables; Bason Stands; Night ditto; Grate, Fire Irons etc.

The bedrooms in the inventory of 1836 included

Mahogany Posted Bedstead with Moreen Curtains and Spring Mattress; elegant French Bed with Curtains and Window Curtain, Hair Mattress and Feather Bed to fit; Bath Blankets and Marseilles Counterpanes; large size Chest Fine Drawers, Secretaire and Wardrobe; double Basin Stand with Stoneware, Toilet Tables and Dressing Glasses ...

There was little change in 1865.

Mahogany Posted Bedstead and Damask Curtains, 3 Feather Beds, Mattresses and Bedding, Chest Mahogany Drawers, Mahogany Toilet Table, Dressing Glass, Chairs, Carpet, Grates.

The basin-stands or toilet-tables usually had a marble top and splash-board, and on them stood a large stoneware ewer and basin. It should be remembered that even in houses with a private wc no washhand basin was provided.

Water-closets appear towards the end of the eighteenth century in tenement houses. One is recorded in a flat in Hutcheson Street, in the New Town, in 1800, flushed from a cistern in the attic which was filled with rain water.[8] At roughly the same time the splendid show house which James Laurie was erecting in Carlton Place to designs by Peter Nicholson boasted no fewer than four wcs — one on each floor — the water for which was pumped up from the basement.[9]

The early wcs were hidden discreetly off a small passage leading to the kitchen or one of the bedrooms, the passage itself being closed off from the lobby by a door. The closet was about five feet square. There was no ventilation. It was to remedy this defect that from the middle of the century the position of the wc was changed to one immediately inside the door, thus enabling a window, or at least a small opening, to be formed to the landing. It was only when bathrooms became common at the end of the century that the enlarged room was lighted and ventilated to the outside by means of a window in the back or front wall.

There were many varieties of treatment, of course, between the primitive single dry-closet in the back-court serving a whole tenement and the provision of a private bathroom in each house. An intermediate stage can be found in 1819, when a superior tenement of six-apartment houses in the city centre had two communal wcs provided in the basement. Bathrooms appear to have come into use at the same time as the wc but were much slower in gaining acceptance, owing to the considerably greater expense involved in providing them. An early example occurs in 1806:

> TO LET THAT GENTEEL & COMMODIOUS LODGING No 52 [VIRGINIA STREET]. . . . The Lodging . . . is accommodated with a neat Flower Plot, a Bath Room, a Cistern for Rain Water, capable of containing nigh three tuns, so that there is at all times a very plentiful supply.[10]

Another example appears in 1836, when a flat at No 3 Bath Street was offered to let at a rent of £38 annually. It contained

> Dining Room, Parlour, Bed Room, Light Bed Closet, Kitchen, 2 Store Closets, Water Closet, on principal floor. In Attics, 4 Bed rooms, Large Closet, and Bath.[11]

The one apartment remaining to be described is the kitchen. Its position varied. In the tenements at Abbotsford Place, it was situated immediately inside the door whereas in other plans, for example, at Grafton Square, it was the furthest apartment from the door. The latter was the more common arrangement, possibly because it meant that the smells of cooking could be better kept under control and were not allowed to assail the nostrils of visitors as soon as they set foot inside the house. The kitchen was invariably at the back of the building in large houses, and the window looked out to the back-court. From the advent of a piped water supply, a sink, or *jawbox*, was fitted into the window recess, with a small cupboard beneath. The water-pipes were of lead or cast-iron in the early days, and the sinks too were frequently of the latter material. Over the sink was the *crane*, a long brass tap shaped like the head and neck of that bird. It was designed in such a way that it could lie horizontal and allow a cover to be placed on top of the sink while not in use.

Beside the window was the larder, a shallow cupboard with shelves and a small window ventilating to the open air. On the gable wall, or sometimes in the corner diagonally opposite the door, the range was fitted. This intricate piece of ironwork was often made to a design patented by a local manufacturer, with names like the 'Hanover' by George McAlpine & Sons, or the 'Excelsior' by Robert Smith & Company, who also produced the 'Globe' open and close fire range and the 'Clutha' portable cooking range. The range contained a small raised fire-basket in the centre, with ash-pan beneath, and an oven on one or both sides with a hotplate above. It often also contained a small boiler for hot water.

Range design reached its climax in the 1890s with elaborate affairs incorporating all possible improvements, and handsomely set off with a surround of coloured tiles in an Art Nouveau pattern. A splendid example of this was the 'Sine qua non' range, described in the following glowing terms by an ironmonger in his advertisement in 1891:

> The great advantage of these ranges is that they can be used either as close or open fire at pleasure. There is no smell of cooking, while in consequence of the bottom grate being adjustable by means of a lever, which raises the fire evenly, bringing the fuel close to the hot plate, a saving of fuel to the extent of quite 50 per cent, is effected. Slow combustion can also be employed, by which means the range can be used for many hours without attention. People who suffer the inconvenience of a smoky chimney will find the 'sine qua non' range a perfect boon. A great difficulty has also been overcome by the makers, namely, providing equal heat at the top and bottom of the oven. Extraordinary heating power can be imparted to the oven and hot plate by means of the patent cold air excluder, fixed at the side of the fire, which has also the advantage of being a smoke consumer.[12]

The predecessor of the range had been a large grate with various forms of apparatus to facilitate cooking — a kitchen of 1804 was described as having 'a Three Wheeled Jack with complete apparatus'. By 1836, however, the embryo range was in existence, for kitchen grates with ovens begin to appear and development was quick from that date. The grate or range, like the grates in the other apartments, was included as a rule in the moveable furniture of the house and was taken by the tenants when they left, along with the fender and jack. After the introduction of gas it became common to have a small ring for cooking placed on one of the hotplates, but this was not until near the end of the century.

Other kitchen fittings included two square cupboards in the largest houses, one for pots, pans, etc and the other used as a coal bunker and store for brushes and other large items. In addition, there were usually shelves along the wall opposite the range. Lighting was provided by a gas lamp on each side of the range. The last, but certainly not the least important feature in the kitchen was the open *bed-recess* which in large houses would be occupied by the cook or resident servant, whose undisputed territory the kitchen was. The iron and wood bed-bottom was built into the recess, which measured roughly six feet by four. Other staff would probably live out, unless there was a basement or attic.

Kitchen furniture was seldom worth listing individually in sale catalogues or valuation inventories, and doubtless was generally of a plain and functional character, although sometimes one could find a valuable but old and unfashionable piece which had been reduced to the status of a working table. In the centre of the room there would be a hardwood table and chairs and, perhaps in a corner, an eight-day or grandfather clock. The 1836 inventory dismisses the kitchen furniture thus:

> Kitchen Grate; Two Chests; Winter Dykes, and Kitchen Utensils.[13]

The floor would usually be covered with oilcloth, with a rug in front of the range.

Such then were the arrangements in a typical large flat. Let us now examine in similar manner a much smaller house, the two-apartment, which was the commonest of all in the later nineteenth century, and was usually referred to as the *Room-and-kitchen*.

The front door, which was neither so wide nor so heavy as in the earlier example, had a plain rectangular fanlight above and led directly into the lobby, which could be either L-shaped or rectangular. Immediately inside was the wc, if an internal one was provided. It was generally tiny, and had a small window to the landing. In the L-plan lobby there were often two presses, fitted in between the Room and kitchen doors and backing on to the bed-recesses. A rectangular lobby would be about 8 feet by 4 feet, while an L-plan lobby would be between 3 ft 6 in and 4 feet wide.

The *Room*, or parlour, was the apartment facing the street. It frequently had a large window about four feet wide, but from the 1870s this often had two lights and measured six or seven feet across. In the 1880s it was further extended to three lights, and then, logically, into a bow or oriel.

The fireplace was in the centre of the gable wall and surmounted by a large timber chimneypiece with a mirror. A press occupied the wall-space between it and the window. A bed-closet was always provided, the built-in bed being hidden from view behind a closed door, an unhygienic arrangement which was forbidden under the provisions of the 1900 Act. From that time, if the closet continued in use for sleeping, the wall in front had to be removed, otherwise it could only be used for storage. The Room was lit by a two- or three-branched gasalier which hung from the centre of the ceiling, which had a moulded centrepiece and cornice. The furniture would not be as elaborate as in the larger houses, leisure being the prerogative of the well-off in Victorian times! Nevertheless, a surprising feature of these small houses, at least in certain districts, was the provision of a bell-pull on each side of the fireplace, for even a house of this size often had a servant. The Room was nearly square as a rule, measuring on average about 13 feet by 12 feet. It may come as a surprise to some readers to discover that in many houses of this size, the Room was hardly ever used. In countless cases, the family lived and slept in the kitchen, the Room being used only on such special occasions as weddings or funerals.

The kitchen was in its customary position at the rear of the building, with a window to the back-court. It was slightly smaller than the Room, being on average about 11 ft 6 in square. The arrangements were similar to those of larger houses, with a sink in the window recess, range and open bed-recess. A small larder was sometimes provided, but a simple, unventilated cupboard was more common. A standard fitting was the combined low cupboard and coal bunker, which occupied a position opposite the range and had two shelves above. The upper shelf ran the whole length of the room, and was usually occupied by the highly polished pots and pans which were not in constant use. The lower shelf ran about three quarters of the length, and was where the dinner service reposed.

In a house of this type, where the family spent almost all their time in the kitchen, the bed-recess contained a built-in bed, usually about 2 ft 6 in above the floor. The space beneath was used for storage and often contained a special bed for the children of the house, which was wheeled, or 'hurled', out at night, hence its common name of *hurley-bed*.

In the 1880s and 1890s it became common for the architect to fit in a scullery off the kitchen. In such cases, the sink was transferred to the scullery window and, with the extra shelving it contained, the scullery became in effect the larder also, while the kitchen assumed more of the character of a living-room. Some architects utilised the space between the scullery and the lobby for the wc and cleverly ventilated the latter to the outside over the scullery's lowered ceiling.

The single-apartment or *single-end*, as it is more familiarly known in Glasgow, was for long the second most popular house-size in the city. Contrary to the implications of its name, it was not found at corners or the ends of passages, but most frequently formed the centre house on a landing containing three. The front door opened into a tiny lobby about four feet square with a press on one side. Only in very rare cases was an internal wc provided in single-ends, but if it was, it occupied a position opposite the press. The latter was the only cupboard accommodation in these houses. A second door opened into the apartment, which was usually of similar size to the Rooms in the adjoining flats, and like them faced the street. The outer wall was occupied by the window, with the sink, and the range. The low cupboard, coal bunker and high shelves were placed on the side wall in front of the door. The bed-recess was fitted into the space behind the door, adjoining the landing. There was no ornamental plasterwork.

Naturally enough, in the second half of last century it was the single-apartment which was the object of particular condemnation by the improvers and health authorities, not because of any inherent faults in its planning but because it attracted the poorest tenants and was as a result frequently overcrowded.[14] The system of ticketing already referred to in Chapter 1 was introduced, with the object of preventing large families from occupying small houses built for single people or childless couples.

1   Its measurements were equally variable. A lobby at 174 New City Road measured overall 35 feet by 12 ft 6 in, while one at 58 Rose Street measured only 16 feet by 11 ft 10 in. A very long, corridor-like lobby at 14 Buccleuch Street measured 33 ft 4 in by 3 ft 10 in.
2   *57 Geo III c 41.* 'An Act for lighting the City and Suburbs of Glasgow with Gas, and for other Purposes relating thereto.'
3   Advertisement in the *Glasgow Herald*, 16 May 1806.
4   *ibid*, 8 May 1865.
5   For details of the College Buildings, see the *Glasgow Herald*, 7 October 1805.
6   Advertisement in the *Glasgow Herald*, 18 April 1836.
7   *ibid*, 2 May 1836.
8   Advertisement in the *Glasgow Courier*, 20 May 1800.
9   Advertisement in the *Glasgow Herald*, 5 December 1808.
10 *ibid*, 16 May 1806.
11 *ibid*, 1 February 1836.
12 Stratten & Stratten Ltd, *Stratten's Glasgow and its Environs — a Literary Commercial and Social Review* (1891) p 166.
13 *Winter dykes* is the old Scottish term for a clothes-horse.
14 There was a considerable difference of quality in single-ends, however. What has been described is a typical example from the 1860s or 1870s. Older ones in back-lands were not so pleasant.

BUILDERS

5
The Tenement Builders

The term 'builder' is used in this chapter in the widest sense, to include not only the contractors who physically erected the buildings but also the individuals and bodies which promoted their erection and the architects who designed them.

As we saw in Chapter 2, the first incentive for the development of a new area for housing came from the owner or immediate superior of the ground who, of course, sometimes was the City Council. It was customary to sell or feu the ground in convenient sized lots, rather than a large area at one time as is done nowadays. This enabled the owner to judge the market for his land and also to obtain a continually rising return on it, as building took place gradually, but regularly. It also encouraged the system of speculative building which played such a prominent part in the development of Victorian Glasgow. Here is an example of such a scheme:

> Some Steadings of building ground in Hutchesontown, similarly situated to such as a few years ago sold at from 4 to 6s per square yard, were on Tuesday last sold by public roup at 8s 9d. The vicinity and ready communication of Hutcheson Town to Glasgow and the Clyde, the beautiful situation of the ground, and the abundant supply of excellent spring water lately found there, may probably be the cause of the great advance of price.[1]

From this we can see how certain parts of the city, popular for one reason or another, began to be quickly purchased and built over at a considerable profit to all concerned. The developments at Tradeston and Laurieston, adjacent to those mentioned above, followed a similar pattern. The seventy-eight acres of Tradeston had been purchased in 1640 by the Trades House for 31 000 merks (£1743.65) and were feued between 1791 and 1856 for £12 425 2s 6d, plus annual feu duties of £4975 18s 10d. In 1831 the highest price obtained had been 3s 6d per square yard, but by 1856 the price had soared to 25s, showing that even at that comparatively early date, city land-prices were becoming inflated.[2]

Building ground in other parts of the city varied very much in price. 759 square yards in Taylor Street, Townhead, was offered for sale in 1808 at 5s per square yard,[3] while 12 963 square yards in Bath Street in the New Town was offered at 8s 6d in 1834.[4] The Trades House, following the success of their Tradeston venture, decided that their property at Sandyford, along the north side of Sauchiehall Street, should not be sold for less than 17s per square yard, although land on the south side of the same street was sold at 15s at the same time.[5]

A small number of proprietors themselves built on their ground, but these were non-profitmaking ventures. Of this class were the Edinburgh and Glasgow Railway Company, with their model village at Cowlairs, and the Glasgow and South Western Railway Company, with theirs at Corkerhill, both outstanding examples of good planning and architecture in the 1860s and 1890s. (See pages 103 and 115.)

In a class apart was the City Improvement Trust, formed by Act of Parliament in 1866 with the avowed object of demolishing substandard houses, improving streets and providing new homes of a high standard for the displaced. It was felt by some that this was the easy answer to all the city's housing problems. But that was certainly not how it turned out. In 1867, a committee was set up to supervise the erection of the first new workmen's dwellings which were planned for the Annfield district. The plans, by the Trust's architect John Carrick, were approved the following year, and tenders were obtained for the work amounting to £4625. The idea was to rehouse about two hundred persons.[6] The cost of acquiring poor and substandard property, however, proved to be a more expensive process than had been anticipated. Instead of building new houses, therefore, the Trust temporarily improved some of its old properties, and even converted one or two cotton mills into single-apartment houses to provide accommodation for the families which were being inevitably displaced by the Trust's other operations.[7] An estimated eighteen hundred people were to be displaced by the redevelopment of the Ingram Street and Bell Street area alone, it was reported in 1870.

As a result of growing criticism of the Trust's failure to implement this section of the Act, a change of policy was advocated in the same year. This involved the purchase of two estates, Overnewton and Oatlands, which were to be feued to speculative builders, who would in turn put up the houses which the Trust itself had so noticeably failed to provide. The Oatlands estate contained 58 638 square yards which were to be laid out in streets and steadings of various sizes, with restrictions regarding the height of the buildings and the minimum area of open ground behind, in order to ensure healthy conditions. When this was done, the ground was to be feued for the immediate erection of dwellings for the labouring classes. These schemes proved so successful that the idea was repeated when the Trust redeveloped Bridgeton and the Gorbals in the period 1872–5. The success, however, was confined to the money-making side of the schemes, for the earlier difficulties were still not overcome by the new method, and in November 1872 the Trust approved that

> A special committee be appointed to enquire into and report how far the operations of the Trust in the destruction of houses of one and two apartments have contributed in raising the rents of old and new workmen's houses throughout the city to their present exorbitant rates, and if it is desirable that the Trust should continue the present mode of pulling down and consequent displacement of tenants occupying small houses, thereby causing an unnatural demand (beyond the power of supply) for workmen's houses resulting in high rents and consequent overcrowding.[8]

The system was simply not working, with the poorest classes still living in wretched conditions, often in lodging-houses, while the better-off tradesmen, always in respectable property, were now being offered even better conditions in a semi-rural setting. But neither the Trust nor the speculative builder could afford to put up houses which they themselves would have to subsidise. The cost of land, as we have already seen, was continually rising — the Trust paid £35 000 for the Overnewton estate — and builders were paying from £4 to £7 10s per square yard for plots in the Gorbals in 1874.

These worries, however, were reduced to insignificance when, on 2 October 1878, the City of Glasgow Bank closed its doors. The effect is described by a contemporary:

> Beyond all doubt the failure of the City of Glasgow Bank ... was the greatest disaster that had ever befallen the commercial community of Great Britain. On its occurrence, the business of the city was paralysed, and as its effects became more and more visible to the public, the panic increased, until there was an almost general collapse.[9]

Many of the builders who had feued land from the Trust were declared bankrupt and building for some time came to a complete standstill. Some builders, trying desperately to struggle on with drastically reduced capital, attempted to obtain sites for reduced prices such as £2 10s per square yard, but were indignantly refused. Nevertheless, recovery was astonishingly quick. By 1882, steadings were selling again in the Gorbals area for £3 10s. In May 1885, Bailie Gray moved

> That it be remitted to the City Architect [John Carrick] to report on an early date, as to the practicability of constructing on the ground of the Improvement Trust (1) Labourers' dwelling houses based on rentals not exceeding 1/3d per room per week. (2) Houses of 1, 2, and 3 apartments for artizans similar to those which have been provided by the Peabody Trustees and others in London and other towns.[10]

The following year, Mr Carrick reported favourably and was instructed to prepare plans of tenements consisting of shops and dwelling-houses, with all modern sanitary arrangements, to be built on ground on the east side of the Saltmarket. The feus on which the tenements were to be built had been previously advertised but with no success. On 15 December 1886, the minutes had recorded that 'no offers have been received from builders regarding vacant sites, therefore the Trustees themselves must undertake to build'. As an experiment, three tenements were to be built on the corner of the Saltmarket and Steel Street, to cost no more than £9000. Thus began the series of model tenements which the Trust was to erect in many different parts of the city, and which will be described in Chapters 8 and 9.

The inability of the City Improvement Trust to provide cheap working-class houses in the 1860s and 1870s prompted the formation of a number of building societies to help people obtain a respectable home for themselves. The first of these was the Glasgow and Suburban Dwellings Company, which built a number of tenements in various parts of the city. They built at Hutcheson Square, Hutchesontown, in Slatefield Street, Camlachie, and at Overnewton, the last buildings containing mostly two-apartment houses. A contemporary organisation was the Glasgow Working Men's Provident Investment Building Society, which built a few tenements of two- and three-apartment houses in Scotland Street and Weir Street, Kingston. A second body with a similar name was the Glasgow Working Men's Investment and Building Society, which concentrated its attention on the south-east. In Springfield Road, Dalmarnock, they erected a range of tenements in 1877, at an estimated cost of £12 000. It contained fourteen shops, nineteen single-apartments, thirty-seven houses of two apartments, and nine houses of three apartments. This society went into voluntary liquidation in 1886.

Besides those mentioned above, there were a number of smaller groups working within restricted areas, such as the Springburn Investment and Building Society, which put up a tenement of three- and four-apartment houses in 1879. But clearly none of these bodies was providing homes for the most needy, the very poor, and it was not until the formation of the Glasgow Workmen's Dwellings Company that housing suitable for them was seriously considered. The company's most important projects, Cathedral Court and Greenhead Court, will be described in Chapter 9, but it should be remembered that, apart from putting up new buildings, the company also reconstructed a number of poor properties, which were by that means made useful for a further period, at far less cost than it would have taken to demolish and rebuild. In this field, they may be said to have been the pioneers.

With the example of the Workmen's Dwellings Company before them, the City Improvement Trust began at last to set aside so many houses in each of their new schemes from the 1890s specifically for the poorest class. From a survey conducted in 1901, we can gather some information about the latest developments, at St James's Road and Haghill.

> Special care has been exercised in letting the houses... so as to secure that the tenants accepted may be of the poorest classes, for whom the buildings are provided. The rule was made that applicants, whose wages did not exceed 26/– should have preference for the houses of two apartments,

and that those whose earnings did not exceed 22/– weekly should be preferred for the single roomed houses.[11]

The tenants of the larger houses were described as belonging to the class of skilled labourers, including engine keepers, cranemen, tanners, forge and iron workers, while the single-apartments were occupied by unskilled labourers. The average rents at that date were £4 16s *per annum* (1s 10d per week) for single-apartments and £11 14s (4s 6d) for a Room-and-kitchen, although at Haghill the rent was only £7 19s, or 3s 1d per week. The cost of these tenements at Haghill was calculated at $4\frac{1}{2}d$ per square foot, including the provision of sinks, ranges and bed fittings.

Important as these ventures were, they provided but a tiny fraction of the great number of tenement houses built in and around the city. The majority were erected by speculative builders financed by private investors, and although many might be masons, wrights, plasterers, or workers in an allied trade, some were simply tradesmen who had decided that house-building was a worthwhile investment. In the latter category were Duncan Fraser, a clothier, who had a shop in Reid Street, Bridgeton and who built about sixty tenements in that area between 1859 and 1876, and James Meikle, who had a dairy in Burnside Street and one of whose ventures will now be examined in detail.

James Meikle built about thirty-three tenements, in three different areas, between 1860 and 1872, including a group at the corner of New City Road and St Peter's Street, St George's Cross. On 18 March 1865, he acquired four steadings of ground there from William Russell, writer, who had previously purchased a larger area of the Blythswood estate which he was now feuing in building lots. The price agreed was 20s per square yard for three of the steadings, and 15s for the fourth, all converted into a ground annual. This was to be paid at Martinmas and Whitsunday, starting at Whitsunday 1866, by which time the tenements could be expected to be finished, if not occupied. The two plots facing New City Road contained 435 and 434 square yards respectively, the one facing St Peter's Street 399 square yards, and the corner plot 778 square yards.

In July 1865 David Thomson, Meikle's architect, prepared a detailed rent-roll based on the plans he had drawn up for the proposed tenements. Number 5 St Peter's Street contained a house of two apartments, annual rent £7, and a single-apartment at £5, both in the basement. The ground floor contained one house of two apartments and one of four apartments, with rents of £9 10s and £19 respectively, while the three upper floors each had two houses of three apartments with a rent of £15 each, the total income for the building being £130 10s. The ground annual was £14 9s 6d. The value of the tenement was calculated as being £1658 when completed; for at that time building was just beginning, the Dean of Guild having approved the plans on 27 April. Similarly, the value of the three other tenements was calculated at £2400, £2264 and £2791, making a total value for the four of £9113.

On this value, Meikle could expect to borrow up to £6000 from properly advised investors. The current rate of interest on well-secured bonds was five per cent. He succeeded in negotiating the necessary loans from four different individuals and secured these by mortgaging the land by the Scottish system of dispositions in security. This meant that the ground and any buildings on it became subject to sale in the event of his default in either the payment of interest or the repayment of capital. As building progressed, the value of the work was reported to the lenders by their valuator (architects were frequently employed for this purpose) and on the production of each certificate of value, part of the promised loan was released. In this way, during 1865 Meikle drew £2900 and eventually borrowed a total amount of £6000 to pay his contractors. Unfortunately, we do not have a record of the building costs of the property or how much Meikle himself contributed. However, the annual income of £737 from rents, after the deduction of £300 of bond interest and £92 18s 10d in ground charges, left £344 1s 2d, to pay for maintenance, insurance and factorage charges, and must have given Meikle a fairly good return for his speculation.

By 1884, we find that the scale of rents had been altered. The two basement houses at No 5 St Peter's Street were now let for £5 each — to Andrew White, mason, and John Roddie, labourer — while the two ground-floor houses had been recon-structed to form two shops and two smaller houses. The shops were let to James Duncan, bootmaker, at £5 and Andrew White, mason, at £25. The houses on the three upper floors had rentals ranging from £15 10s to £17, and were occupied by two joiners, a spirit salesman, a traveller and a dyer. Occupants of the adjoining properties included a hairdresser, two plumbers, a grocer who also had his shop in the building, a bookseller and a railway guard. Their houses faced New City Road, and they paid rents rather higher than those already noticed, ranging from £18 to £19 15s. The highest rent of all came from a public house on the corner, which paid £99.

In 1908, we find that the rents have not changed very much. The basement houses are valued at £4 15s and £6 10s, those on the ground floor at £10 10s and £9 18s; and those on the upper flats at £16 10s, with the exception of one on the top floor which is only £16. It is interesting that one of the basement householders could only afford 1s 10d towards his half-year's rent in that year — a foretaste of the difficult period ahead. In 1901, the half yearly statement informs us that £492 17s 9d was collected in rent. Expenses included £48 9s 11d in taxes, maintenance costs of £35 3s 3d, and £12 8s 5d in factorage expenses. £146 4s 11d was paid in 'heritable burdens', including £99 15s interest on the bonds of 1865 and 1866, and £14 5s 2d in insurance, covering fire, accidents and the plate glass. Further investigation of these properties after 1910 is pointless, owing to the effect on builders' and investors' profits first of taxation changes, and then of state rent and mortgage controls. All four tenements, after standing derelict for some time, were demolished in 1974.

Among other tenement builders of the 1860s and 70s, we find a strange assortment, including John Keddie, carter; Peter Dixon, cowfeeder; John Law, baker; James Richmond, tinsmith; John Burt, leather merchant; and Thomas Philp, whose firm was described as being stair-railers, fret-cutters, carvers, plain and ornamental turners, and Bowling Green bowl-makers! Tradesmen like these were in a minority, of course, and the really serious work of tenement building was undertaken by the professional builders. In the first half of the nineteenth century these were differentiated as being either masons or wrights, but gradually those who did building construction were termed *builders*, while the *masons* were stone cutters, and the *wrights* concentrated on the timberwork alone.

In the *Post Office Directory* for 1824, no fewer than forty-four builders are listed, and there is evidence to show that this was not the total number then practising in the city. James Cruikshank, in his history of the masons, made the total fifty. [12] He points out, however, that several of them were only 'taskers', *ie* masons who contracted to do the hewn work of a building as piece-work under the main contractor. A few examples may be cited of that period.

The largest firm belonged to Alexander Garden, who had 187 masons employed in building in the central area between Hope Street and Blythswood Square. It is reported that he cut off no less than thirty feet from the top of the hill in order to form the square. He subcontracted much of his work, but later, owing to his slowness in paying his bills, he found it necessary to employ his men by the day.

Because of the large amount of work he was doing, he was accused of causing the level of wages to rise from 20*s* to 24*s*, and even to 27*s* in 1825, with the customary seasonal drop to 17*s* in winter. Garden's business collapsed at that time and it is significant that the masons' wages did not rise at all the following summer, but remained at 17*s*.

A number of builders worked their own quarries in and around the city. Among these was Robert Aitken, who had a large business, although he only employed thirty-five masons. His quarry, which yielded a large quantity of very fine white rock suitable for frontages, was at the top of Buchanan Street, on the east side. There were five cranes in the quarry, each worked by a team of four men. Another builder of the same period was John Taylor. In 1826 he built a tenement in Portland Street which collapsed in a gale, causing a great deal of damage. Despite the fact that he had previously employed fifty men, from that time he ceased to build on his own account.[13]

The expansion of the building trade during the second half of the nineteenth century was exceptional. The *Post Office Directory* for 1840 lists 107 builders, that for 1860, 180; and those for 1882 and 1899, 238. As this was the great period of housing expansion in and around the city, many of these builders specialised in tenements. George and Alexander Eadie are typical examples. From the 1860s they erected a large number of tenements, beginning in Hutchesontown and then moving southwards to the new suburbs of Govanhill and Mount Florida.

A variation on the stonemason-builder was the brickmaker who also indulged in building. This was a very convenient combination, for by the second half of the century brick was very largely used in tenement construction, often only the front and back walls being of stone. William Steven and John Porter were two of these brickmaker-builders. Steven began business in 1840, Porter somewhat later, having taken over his father's brickmaking firm and expanded it to include building. Both built in the east end, chiefly in Bridgeton and Dalmarnock.

The role of the architect in tenement design has not been fully appreciated; in fact it has been stated that they did not design tenements at all! Contrary to this belief, however, there is indisputable evidence that almost all the Glasgow architects designed tenements as a normal part of their practice. The dividing line between an architect and builder in the late eighteenth century is sometimes difficult to detect, and many obviously acted as both. One of the best-known of these was Robert Smith, who was responsible for many of the buildings in the New Town, in Glassford Street, Hutcheson Street and George Square.[14]

Specialisation did not really take effect until the Victorian age, when many builders encouraged their sons to take a step up the social ladder and become architects. The most notable of these was probably Charles Wilson, who always declared himself grateful for the practical grounding he had received in his father's workshop. His contribution to tenement design was considerable. His grasp of proportion and sensitivity to architectural ornament are clearly seen in all his elevations. The tenements which can be confidently attributed to him are all of a superior type and sited in prestige areas such as Garnethill, Sandyford or Laurieston, and it is possible that with such a busy practice he only accepted the more important commissions. Wilson's successor David Thomson, on the other hand, built up a reputation for himself by designing a considerable number of tenements of a superior working-class type, at Gorbals Cross and in the area around St George's Cross. These were distinguished by good internal planning rather than by elaboration of external detail.[15]

John Baird I was in great demand as a tenement designer. He was involved in Monteith Row, and also parts of Laurieston and Woodside, providing plans for both the middle and working class. He seems to have been the pioneer of the rectangular stair which became so popular later in the century.[16] Baird's successor, James Thomson I, continued on the same lines, finding time in what was probably the busiest practice in Victorian Glasgow to design many varied types of tenement. He was constantly employed by a number of builders for their schemes, in almost every part of the city. For superior examples, and those on prestige sites along main streets such as Argyle Street or Gorbals Street, he provided fairly elaborate variations on the Italian palace theme. He also worked closely with the City Improvement Trust, being responsible for the tenements surrounding the newly-cleared Bridgeton Cross in 1871.[17]

Alexander Kirkland's plans for the development of the Stobcross estate (St Vincent Crescent, with Corunna and Minerva Streets), were among the most ambitious and splendid of their kind. In elevational treatment Kirkland followed Wilson's lead in using Italian Renaissance with projecting porches. His plans, however, were quite different from Wilson's and he often used the Edinburgh custom of having the stair at the front of the building.[18] Kirkland's work will be discussed again in Chapter 7.

John Burnet was another important architect, and a block of his most striking tenements is illustrated in Fig 8 on p 89, but it should be remembered that he designed many others of equal interest, but with simpler frontages, for example in Hillhead.[19] John Burnet's son, John James Burnet, also designed some fine tenements during the course of a distinguished career. They include what was probably the most expensive, as well as the most spectacular block in the city — Charing Cross Mansions, which he designed with his partner John A Campbell (see p 105 and Plate 40). It should not be forgotten, however, that Burnet was also capable of working in a much simpler style, for example the two courts of flats for the Workmen's Dwellings Company described on p 112ff.[20]

James Salmon's contribution was equally varied. He provided high amenity flats in Dennistoun but also designed many working-class ones in Plantation. The internal planning was always carefully thought out, as befitted one who prided himself on a knowledge of hygiene.[21]

The only really original contribution to tenement design, however, was that of Alexander Thomson, who revolutionised the standard elevation by linking its isolated elements in a manner at once masterly, and entirely his own.[22] This can be seen in the contemporary but vastly different examples in Eglinton Street and Paisley Road West, the latter severe almost to a fault and the former exuberant in an abundance of clever detail. 'Greek' Thomson's highly individual contribution will be dealt with in more detail in Chapter 7.

The important work of these architects was, by its nature, limited. Not many developers or builders could afford outstanding buildings of the kind these architects produced, and so the plans of lesser men were used. Chief among these was J C McKellar, whose firm designed some 640 tenements within the city boundary between 1890 and 1910. All were of red sandstone with bows or oriels, and often formed considerable areas in themselves, *eg* Langside and Hyndland.[23] Another prolific firm was Burnet and Boston (no relation of the Burnets referred to above), which turned out designs for about 540 tenements between 1884 and 1906, including the elaborate ranges built in the High Street and Woodlands Road for the Improvement Trust.

One phenomenon of the latter part of the nineteenth century was the appearance on the scene of a group of architects who specialised in the design of tenements to the almost complete exclusion of everything else. These may be called the tenement architects, and among the small one-man firms of this kind was George F Boyd, who produced no fewer than 354 plans between 1886 and 1911; another was John Nisbet, who produced 230 plans between 1895 and 1909, many for John A Mactaggart, a builder who was to rise to prominence after World War I with the building of garden suburbs, but who began in the traditional way. Other tenement designers were John Grant Sharp, of the house-factors Sharp and Fairlie, who designed some 260 tenements between 1880 and 1924; and John Short, who started as clerk of works to various builders, began building on his own account and finally reached the status of an architect, designing 210 tenements in the short period between 1892 and 1899. A considerable list could be compiled of similar men, who took advantage of the opportunities offered by the building boom in the years of prosperity between 1882 — when the city recovered from the effects of the City Bank crash — and 1910, when the great age, the golden age of the tenement in Glasgow, came to an end.

1 In the *Glasgow Herald*, 18 October 1805.
2 Crawfurd, *Sketch ... of the Trades' House* p 187. A merk was worth two-thirds of a Scots pound which is here valued at $1s\,8\frac{1}{4}d$ sterling (just under 8.5p).
3 Advertisement in the *Glasgow Herald*, 28 March 1808.
4 Advertisement in the *Glasgow Courier*, 3 April 1834.
5 Crawfurd, *Sketch ... of the Trades' House* p 209.
6 *Minutes of the Glasgow City Improvement Trust*, 26 November 1867, 17 March 1868 and 28 September 1868.
7 *ibid*, 4 May 1869 and 25 January 1870.
8 *ibid*, 14 November 1872.
9 G MacGregor, *The History of Glasgow* (1881) p 493.
10 *Minutes of the Glasgow City Improvement Trust*, 20 May 1885.
11 A Kay, *The Corporation of Glasgow as Owners of Shops, Tenements and Warehouses* (1902) p 10.
12 J Cruikshank, *A Sketch of the Incorporation of Masons* (1879). The author, himself a mason, gives much information and many anecdotes about Glasgow builders in the nineteenth century.
13 *ibid*, pp 76 and 94.
14 Advertisements in the *Glasgow Courier*, 8 November 1791 and 21 November 1795.
15 Charles Wilson, 1810–1863; David Thomson, 1831–1910.
16 John Baird I, 1798–1859 (see Plate 21).
17 James Thomson I, 1835–1905.
18 Alexander Kirkland, c1824–1892.
19 John Burnet, 1814–1901.
20 John James Burnet, 1857–1938.
21 James Salmon, 1805–1888 (see Plate 21).
22 Alexander 'Greek' Thomson, 1817–1875 (see Plate 21).
23 John Campbell McKellar, 1859–1941.

BUILDINGS

6
Before 1800

When the continental form of house building typified by the tenement — vertical rather than horizontal — began to appear on the streets of the burghs, it was not something totally new to the Scottish scene. The castles and fortified tower-houses to be found in all parts of the country were designed on a similar plan, with one room above another and connected by a single stair. They were even of roughly the same height, the towers containing usually three stories and an attic, which corresponds remarkably closely to the four stories of the Victorian tenement. Although the tower-houses may be considered essentially rural architecture, by the latter half of the sixteenth century buildings of similar plan and appearance were to be found in many of the more important burghs, including Glasgow. One author has given a description of the city at that date:

> The main thoroughfare, stretching from the Market Cross to the Cathedral Church, had dwellings and booths on each side, the number on the west preponderating, as on the opposite side considerable space was taken up by the Blackfriars Convent and College buildings and grounds. Southward from the Cross a street extended to the South Port and then branched off obliquely towards the bridge. Again starting from the Cross the Gallowgait extended eastward a little beyond the Molendinar Burn, and the

Trongait westward, with a prolongation towards St Tenu's Chapel. There were few buildings in the Gallowgait on the east side of the Molendinar, while those on the north side of the Trongait did not extend farther than the West Port. There were a few houses in Stockwellgait, and a turreted building at the northwest corner. At least one wynd extended from Trongait to Bridgegait, and there were also wynds or vennels on each side of the High Street. From the Wyndhead ... the Ratounraw branched out on the west and the Drygait on the east, and these streets were largely occupied by the dwellings of church dignitaries. ... A few isolated dwellings might be scattered here and there beyond the range of the streets above enumerated, but, subject to such exceptions, the built area of the city was confined within the limits indicated. Dr Cleland, in his Statistical Account of Glasgow, estimated that the population of the town at the time of the Reformation amounted to about 4500.[1]

Only one domestic building of this early date survives. This is Provand's Lordship in Castle Street, which was erected *circa* 1471 by Bishop Andrew Muirhead as the domestic portion of St Nicholas' Hospital.[2] It is a stone rubble-built structure of three stories and attic and presents a deceptively modern appearance when viewed from the street. It measures 53 ft 9 in by 24 ft and is divided internally into three equal-sized rooms on each floor, reached originally by means of a projecting stair-tower and timber balconies. These were probably removed when the present stair was constructed and various other additions made to convert the building into a tenement. The date 1670 is incised on a skew-putt of the addition.

Edinburgh has a much better record than Glasgow for preserving its early buildings, and one must examine examples there to find out what was happening at this date. One very well-known example, the tenement known as John Knox's House, can still be seen at 45 High Street. The original structure dates from *circa* 1545, but has been continually added to over the following half-century or so, giving a particularly good idea of the piecemeal development of housing during that period. There are three stories, attic and basement and, like Provand's Lordship, John Knox's House appears to have had three apartments on each floor. The building in this case, however, is at right angles to the street, to which it presents a narrow frontage of only about 26 feet. The upper floors are reached by two turnpike stairs, one near the centre of the building, and the other entering from a forestair.[3]

In Glasgow, the earliest real tenement to be recorded stood at 138 Trongate and had a stone with the date 1591 built into it. McUre, in 1736, refers to this building as 'the great tenement belonging to the heirs of Michael Coulter, late bailie'. Small's view of 1885 shows a four-storied tenement with three crow-stepped gables surmounted by chimneys facing the street. Previous to 1800, it apparently had only two gablets, and the date-stone formed the skew-putt of one of them. As that was the common position for such stones, it would seem that the building as it survived in 1800 was in its original form. The reconstruction which took place then completely altered its appearance. In addition to three new shopfronts, the windows on the first and second floors were enlarged and provided with wooden entablatures. The third-floor windows seem to have remained untouched. The original appearance of this building, with its two gablets, shows that the slightly continental influence which was to be found in the architecture of the east coast was to be found in the west also.[4]

Despite their dates, these two sixteenth-century examples are hardly typical of the great majority of burgh buildings at that time, being obviously superior specimens. Most tenements were still only two stories and an attic in height, with timber galleries at front or back, and often with the space beneath the front gallery boarded in to form a *booth* or shop. Buildings of that kind certainly stood on the Bell o' the Brae in the High Street, and at the foot of the Saltmarket.[5] Most houses at that time had only two living apartments, referred to as the *hall* and *chamber*.

> DISPOSITION by JAMES LIES, merchant, burgess of Glasgow, to the burgh of Glasgow, of a void space which was (before being burnt fifty-two years since) a tenement of land containing a hall and chamber on the east side of the High Street, near the Stinking Vennel, above the well there, 'now in building be the toune'.[6] (1656)

The houses appear also to have been sparsely furnished. One, in Edinburgh in 1530, contained only the following furniture: a counter (table), a furnished bed, an aumbry (cupboard), a chair and a form.[7]

With the prosperity of the early seventeenth century came an improvement in the architectural appearance of burgh buildings.

FRONT ELEVATION

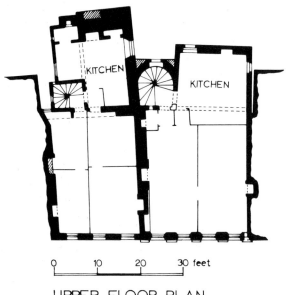

UPPER FLOOR PLAN

Figure 1 17–27 High Street, of the early seventeenth century. It can be seen from the plan that the original hall-and-chamber accommodation of the upper floors has been subdivided at a later date with wooden partitions. Two of the rooms thus created have no window.

Timber galleries were no longer built, but their place was taken by stone-built projections with an open arcade at street level. In Glasgow, buildings of this kind were a feature of the High Street, Trongate and Saltmarket, where they were much admired by visitors. Most were four stories and an attic in height, with crow-stepped gables, and built of ashlar freestone. The arcades, or *piazzas* as they were called, provided a practical and attractive roofed shopping area, while the upper floors contained convenient and commodious dwelling-houses. By this period ideas of comfort were changing rapidly. The principal rooms now had painted timber ceilings, or even decorative plaster ones. The walls would be painted, panelled, or hung with tapestry. Contemporary records describe houses of this period as having halls, chambers, galleries, attics, cellars, kitchens and stables. In 1635 a flat in Chalmers' Close, Edinburgh, was described as consisting of a hall, chamber, kitchen and back stair — the equivalent of a better-class three-apartment house of parlour, bedroom and kitchen in later days.[8]

The last examples of this type of tenement in Glasgow stood at 17 and 27 High Street, and were demolished by the City Improvement Trust in the 1870s. Luckily, measured drawings were made of them before demolition took place.[9] Number 17 had a street frontage of only about 21 feet, but extended back 50 feet. It was four stories and attic in height, the front elevation consisting of a two-arched piazza at ground level, with three windows in each of the floors above, the whole completed with a steeply pitched gable. Each floor contained five apartments, probably divided between two houses, entered from a square turnpike stair near the back of the building.

The tenement to the north, No 27, also of four stories and attic, was apparently of slightly later date than No 17, as it had higher ceilings and more generous window-space. On the front elevation it had three arches at ground level, with four windows in each of the upper floors, terminating in two crow-stepped gablets, each having a dormer window of similar size to those below. At the time of the survey both buildings had been much altered and it is not easy to work out the original arrangements. It seems likely that the upper floors, like those of its neighbour, were divided into two houses, of two and three apartments respectively, reached by a circular turnpike stair accommodated in a squared projection between the two buildings.

Edinburgh, besides having many more surviving seventeenth-century tenements than Glasgow, is also the subject of a remarkable bird's-eye view made by James Gordon of Rothiemay in 1647, showing all the buildings then existing in considerable detail. For example, the north side of the High Street is shown with the roofs of the long rows of back-lands stretching behind the street tenements.[10] Clearly, in the capital all available ground had been built over by that date. Unfortunately, no such detailed view of Glasgow was made until the mid-nineteenth century. There are, however, two views of the city from selected vantage points by Captain John Slezer, who visited Glasgow *circa* 1690. These show buildings, mostly two stories in height, dominated by a group of fine seventeenth-century steeples.[11] Neither view, however, shows the city centre, where the highest and most interesting buildings were to be found.

During the seventeenth century, two disastrous fires destroyed considerable areas of the city. The first took place on 17 June 1652 and, occurring during the puritanical days of Cromwell's Commonwealth, was ascribed to Divine displeasure! It began in one of the narrow closes on the east side of the High Street and, fanned by a north-east wind, quickly spread southwards to the Trongate, Gallowgate, Saltmarket and Bridgegate, raging for eighteen hours and destroying the homes of almost a thousand families.[12] Following this disaster, the magistrates and council were quick to control the rebuilding which would inevitably take place.

> It is statute and ordainet that nae windskews or hallens [kinds of projecting screens or canopies] above doir heidis be sufferit to be put out heirefter, and that the deane of gild present and to come tack speciall notice therof, except that it fall out that some buithes be betwixt twa hinging stairis, in that cais the awneris of which buithes ar licentiat to put out ane windskew or hallen above thair buith doirs, bot the samyne to come no farder out nor the saids hinging stairs sall be.... And seeing now that the maist pairt of the foir landis in Saltmercat will be re-edifeit againe, it is statute and ordainet that nae maner of persoune be sufferrit to come farder out then another, and that all houssis on both the sydes of the gait be buildit conform to ane straicht lyne. ...[13]

It was also decided to send one James Colquhoun to Edinburgh in 1656, to look at that city's fire-engine — the first in Scotland. On his return it was agreed to build a similar 'ingyne for casting of water on land that is in fyre' for the use of Glasgow in future emergencies.[14] The new 'ingyne' does not seem to have been of much use, however, during the second great fire.

November 3 1677, the fire brake up in Glasgow, in the heid

of the Saltmercat, on the right near the cross, which was kyndled by a malicious boy, a smith's apprentice, who being threttned, or beat & smitten by his master, in revenge whereof setts his workhouse on fyre in the night tyme, being in the backsides of that fore street, and flyes for it. It was kyndled about one in the morning; and having brunt many in the backsyd, it breaks forth in the fore streets about three of the morning; and then it fyres the street over against it and in a very short tyme burned down to more than the mids of the Saltmercat on both sydes, fore and back houses were all consumed. ... The heat was so great that it fyred the horologe of the tolbooth (there being some prisoners in it at that tyme ... the people brake open the tolbooth doors and sett them free).... It was a great conflagration and nothing inferior to that which was in the yeir 1652. The wind changed several times. Great was the cry of the poor people, and lamentable to see their confusion.[15]

Losses must have been considerable, for one merchant, John Gilhagie, claimed to have lost 20 000 merks (£1111.11).

As in 1652, the authorities took the opportunity to control the manner of rebuilding, and on 4 December 1677 announced that

... they out of their dewtie to sie to the preservatioune of their burgh and citie, doe statut and ordaine that quhen it sall pleas God to put any of their nighbouris in ane capacitie and resolutioune to build *de novo*, or repair their ruinous houssis, not only for their probable securitie but als for decoring the said burgh, that each persone building *de novo* on the hie streit, or repairing, sall be obleidged and is heirby obleist to doe it by stone work, from heid to foot, bak and foir, without ony timber or daill [boarding] except in the insett thereof, quhilk is understood to be partitions, doors, windowes, presses and such lyk ...[16]

On 9 October 1678 one Alexander Thom, 'architectour', was granted liberty and licence to reside within the burgh and to carry on his calling in 'architectorie or in measonrie' — the first Glasgow architect to be recorded.[17] Obviously much rebuilding was taking place. Apparently regulations were not enough to ensure suitable rebuilding, and in 1699 the magistrates and town council resorted to straightforward bribery. Where a property was rebuilt completely of stone and with a slate roof, the owner was to be free from taxation for the following ten years![18]

Perhaps the most celebrated tenement of the late seventeenth century was the one known as Gibson's Land. McUre, in 1736, describes it as

> The great and stately tenement of land built by the deceast Walter Gibson merchant and late provost of Glasgow, standing upon eighteen stately pillars or arches, and adorn'd with the several orders of architecture, conform to the direction of that great architect Sir William Bruce, the entry consists of four several arches towards the court thereof: this magnificent structure is admir'd by all foreigners and strangers.[19]

Its end was dramatic.

> On the morning of Sunday, 16 February 1823 the great tenement fronting the Saltmarket and Prince's Street, known by the name of Gibson's Land, fell into the Saltmarket and Prince's Street with a tremendous crash, carrying part of the opposite corner tenement in Prince's Street along with it. It is almost miraculous that in such a catastrophe one man only lost his life.[20]

Luckily, on the preceding evening, the inhabitants had been warned to leave the building by the Dean of Guild. The scare which resulted from this incident caused the demolition, often quite unnecessarily, of a number of the city's oldest buildings.

The eighteenth century saw a logical development of the ideas tentatively tried in the last decade of the previous century. Under the influence of architects like Bruce, Mylne and William Adam, the old Scottish vernacular style, with its corbie-steps and dormer windows, began to disappear amid the new sophistication of city life. Tenements now contained houses of greater size, and with a corresponding increase in comfort. Houses of five apartments were now common, and sometimes even eleven apartments could be found when a house occupied more than one floor. In Glasgow, a house in Bell's Wynd was exposed for sale in 1766 — 'the third Storie is possessed by Mr Connel, Dean of Guild, consisting of four Rooms, a Kitchen, and two Garret Rooms'.[21] In the same year another advertisement, in the *Glasgow Journal*, announces:

> To be sold, ... Two Stories of that large Tenement of Land newly Built by John Shortridge, lying on the South side of

Argyll Street, each Story consisting of a Kitchen and Eight
Fire Rooms, with Closets to most of the Rooms, and Two
large Cellars, and a Garret room to each story. ... The
Rooms and Presses are all well Lighted, the Braces
[chimneypieces] and Bedplaces well Disposed: Two
Rooms in each Story have Private Doors from the Stair-
Head for Writing-Rooms or Kitchens; and each Story is
laid out so as to serve Two Families if needful. Several of
the Rooms are large and the Roof high, and at the head of
the Closs there is a private Well with very fine soft Water.[22]

Such were the houses of the middle classes, and they were finished
with a considerable degree of elegance. The rent would be about 100
pounds Scots (£8.33).

A description of the city in the early part of the century was
published by Daniel Defoe in 1727, where he says:

Glasgow is the emporium of the west of Scotland, being,
for its commerce and riches, the second in this northern
part of Great Britain. It is a large, stately, and well-built
city, standing on a plain, in a manner four square; and the
four principal streets are the fairest for breadth, and the
finest built that I have ever seen in one city together. The
houses are all built of stone, and generally uniform in
height, as well as in front. The lower stories, for the most
part, stand on vast square Doric columns, with arches,
which open into the shops, adding to the strength, as well as
beauty of the building. In a word 'tis one of the cleanliest,
most beautiful, and best-built cities in Great Britain.[23]

This was praise indeed.

Defoe's visit coincided with the beginnings of the new trade and
prosperity which were going to put Glasgow on the world map. The
free trade with the American colonies was to be the source of the city's
wealth for the following century. Indicative of the new prosperity are
the population figures, which rose from about 12 500 in 1707, the date
of the Union of Parliaments, to 19 000 in mid-century, and to 62 000
by 1790.

Edward Burt was another visitor about the same time, and his
impressions were similar.

The houses are faced with ashlar stone; they are well
sashed, all of one model, and piazzas rise round them on
either side, which gives a good air to the buildings. There

are some handsome streets; but the extreme parts of the
town are mean and disagreeable to the eye.[24]

McUre, the city's first historian, gives an idyllic picture of the place:

... surrounded with cornfields, kitchen and flower
gardens, and beautiful orchyards, abounding with fruits of
all sorts, which, by reason of the open and large streets,
send forth a pleasant odoriferus smell.[25]

However, as a later author puts it:

Beside the substantial houses of the well-to-do citizens,
with quaint picturesque Flemish architecture and crow-

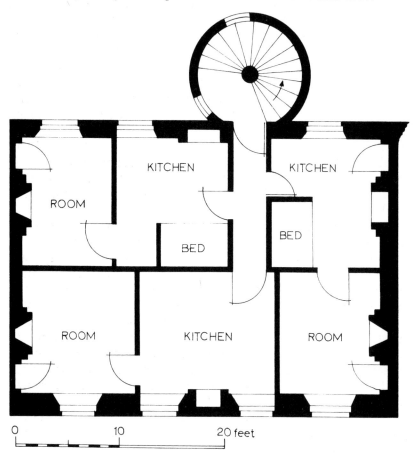

Figure 2 394 Gallowgate, a three-storied tenement of 1771. Upper floor plan. The front
elevation of this building was similar to Plate 23.

stepped gables, ... stood mean, dirty, and broken-down
hovels to mar the beauty of the town; while in the streets
stood middens, against which magistrates vainly objected,
and in the gutters remained garbage seriously to spoil the
'odoriferus smell' of the fruit and flower-scented air.[26]

Glasgow has no remaining tencment from the first half of the
century, and only a few from the second. As might be expected, these
examples are of better-class structures, the poorer ones having been
swept away long ago. Most of the remaining buildings are to be found
in the New Town, which grew up as a direct result of the American and
West Indian trade. It spread east and west beyond the old city ports,
which were demolished in 1754 and 1751 respectively.

In the area beyond the East Port, two tenements survive at 374 and
394 Gallowgate. Number 374 is three stories in height with a small
central pediment supporting a chimney-head, and has the rusticated
quoins typical of late eighteenth-century buildings. Each floor has six
apartments divided, possibly at a later date, into three houses of two
apartments each, two back-to-back and one through-and-through.
Entrance is by a close near the centre of the building, leading through
to the foot of the staircase tower. Number 394 was built in 1771 and
has three stories and attics, with an attractive nepus gable containing
two windows, but also supporting a chimney-head. There are also
rusticated quoins and rolled skew-putts. The accommodation is
similar to that of its neighbour.

That splendid example of new-found civic pride and prosperity, St
Andrew's Parish Church, was built in the middle of the century. The
projected square around it, however, had to wait another fifty years
before completion. Sections of the north and east sides still remain to
give an idea of what must have been one of the most attractive parts of
the city when in its prime. In 1795 the centre tenement on the east side
was advertised for sale. We learn that the cellars, ground and first
floors were occupied as business premises by two firms of
manufacturers, each having four large rooms. The top floor consisted
of a large dining-room fronting the Square, an elegant drawing-room
fronting the Green, two bedrooms and a kitchen. The drawing-rooms
on the east and south sides of the Square had bow windows with an
open outlook over the city's only public park.[27] The northern side,
like the others, has a fairly uniform frontage, with a pediment on the
central block.

The main movement of city development, however, was westward.
Mention has already been made, in Chapter 1, of that portion of the

New Town occupied by the merchant class and largely consisting of villas. Nevertheless, the greater part of the development took the traditional form of tenements, and some of these can still be seen in the Candleriggs and Glassford Street.

The most important New Town tenement to survive until recent times was Spreull's Land, No 182 Trongate, which was built in 1784.

> No such tenement as Spreull's Land had ever been erected in Trongate — or, for the matter of that, in Glasgow — before, and for years its spiral hanging 'well' staircase was reckoned one of the sights of the city. It was originally designed for shops below and dwelling-houses of a highly superior order (for a 'land') above ...[28]

The elliptical hanging stair in the centre of the building was certainly its outstanding feature, and was entered from a wide, arched

Figure 3   Spreull's Land, No 182 Trongate, built in 1784. The arched pend led to the central stair and the court behind. In its last days, the building had lost its window-mouldings.

pend which also gave access to the court behind (Plate 24). Each of the three upper floors had two houses, each containing five main apartments, a large lobby and a number of smaller rooms or closets. The drawing-rooms at the back of the building overlooking the court had wide segmental bows lit by three windows, similar to those at St Andrew's Square. Spreull's Land, like most of its contemporaries, fell victim to the devotees of so-called progress and improvement, and was demolished in 1978.

Although the architect of Spreull's Land is unknown, there is the possibility that it was designed by Robert or James Adam, whose contribution to both Edinburgh and Glasgow architecture at this period was outstanding. The Trades House in the heart of Glasgow's New Town is their work, and it seems likely that they were involved in other contemporary projects in the same area. Certainly, James Adam was commissioned by the University to design a new housing development for them opposite the old college buildings in the High Street. This involved the opening up of a new street, appropriately named College Street, on the corners of which the first and most elaborate buildings were erected in 1794–5. In November of the latter year an advertisement appeared in the *Glasgow Courier*:

> HOUSES TO BE LET, IN THE NEW BUILDING OPPOSITE TO THE COLLEGE, GLASGOW.
> The attick storry, consisting of a dining-room, a drawing-room, four bed-rooms, a kitchen, a larder, a servants bed-room, and two closets, all on the same floor; also five garret bed-rooms, and a closet, the entry to ditto by an inside stair. The first flat, south side, consisting of a dining-room, a drawing-room, five bed-rooms, a kitchen, a larder, a servants bed-room, a light dressing-closet, and four dark closets. The first flat, north side, consisting of a large shop or warehouse, three rooms, a kitchen, a larder, and two closets.[29]

These two buildings, which in fact were the only part of the scheme to materialise, were of three stories and attics and of similar elevational treatment. The end bays of the first and second floors were contained within a giant Corinthian Order. The pilasters and engaged columns supported a massive cornice extending across the whole façade, forming a bold and original treatment of Classical elements typically Adam in concept. In the 1970s these outstanding buildings were suddenly declared to be unsafe and, despite protest from various interested parties, were demolished.

1 R Renwick (ed), *Abstract of Protocols of the Town Clerks of Glasgow* (11 vols, 1894–1900) vol I, p xiii. See also Plate 1.
2 W Gemmell, *The Oldest House in Glasgow* (1910), gives a complete history and description of the building.
3 See *Inventory of the Ancient and Historical Monuments of the City of Edinburgh* (1951) pp 96–99, where a very full description will be found.
4 D Small and A H Millar, *Sketches of Quaint Bits in Glasgow* (1887) VIII.
5 For illustrations of these see R Stuart, *Views and Notices of Glasgow in Former Times* (1848) pp 63–66, and also Annan, No 25.
6 Marwick, *Charters and Other Documents, 1649–1707* p 318. The disposition is dated 28 August, 1656.
7 *Inventory of . . . Edinburgh*, p lxvii.
8 *ibid*, p lxviii.
9 *The British Architect*, 1 September 1876.
10 See *Inventory of . . . Edinburgh*, pp 45 and 91, where sections are reproduced.
11 Stuart, *Views and Notices* pp 1 and 5.
12 See J D Marwick and R Renwick (eds), *Extracts from the Records of the Burgh of Glasgow* (11 vols, 1876–1916), *1630–1662* p 229 for contemporary details of the fire.
13 *ibid, 1630–1662* p 233 (3 July 1652).
14 *ibid, 1630–1662* p 344.
15 From Law's Memorials, quoted in J McUre, *The History of Glasgow* (1736, new ed 1830) p 123.
16 Marwick [and Renwick], *Extracts from the Records of the Burgh of Glasgow, 1663–1690* p 244.
17 *ibid, 1663–1690* p 259.
18 *ibid, 1691–1717* pp 283–4.
19 McUre, *History* p 126 (1830 ed).
20 Gordon, *Glasghu facies* vol 1, p 454.
21 *ibid*, vol 1, p 443.
22 *ibid*, vol 2, p 1027.
23 Quoted in McUre's *History* p 310 (1830 ed).
24 H G Graham, *The Social Life of Scotland in the 18th Century* (5th ed 1969) p 131.
25 McUre, *History* p 122 (1830 ed).
26 Graham, p 131.
27 Advertisement in the *Glasgow Courier*, 19 February 1795. See Plate 27.
28 'Senex' and others, *Glasgow Past and Present* (3 vols, 1884) vol III, p 475.
29 Advertisement in the *Glasgow Courier*, 5 November 1795.

Plate 21   Above, John Baird I, 1798–1859—taken from *Memoirs and Portraits of One Hundred Glasgow Men* (1886) vol I, no VII; James Salmon, 1805–1888—from *The Bailie,* no 2. *Below,* John Carrick, 1819–1890, first City Architect—from *The Bailie,* no 74; Alexander 'Greek' Thomson, 1817–1875—frontispiece to *The British Architect* vol III (1875).

Plate 22 (right) 'The Oldest House in the Trongate'. David Small's drawing of No 138 Trongate (see p 63) as it was in the 1800s.

Plate 23 (below) A late eighteenth-century tenement, No 384—388 Gallowgate, *c* 1900. The nepus gable, rusticated quoins and rolled skew-putts of this building make it a typical example of its period.

Plate 24 (far right) One of the city's most idiosyncratic ranges of tenements, Balmoral Crescent, Crosshill.

HOLYROOD JOHN McELROY. VAULTS.

Plate 25 Annan: Main Street, Gorbals, 1868. The rural atmosphere of the old village is still in evidence here.

Plate 26 Crown Street looking north from Ballater Street, *c* 1900. The exceptional spaciousness of the streets of the new Gorbals is obvious from this view of the main thoroughfare of Hutchesontown. It can be seen that this was not yet a poverty-stricken area, and the inhabitants were largely middle-class.

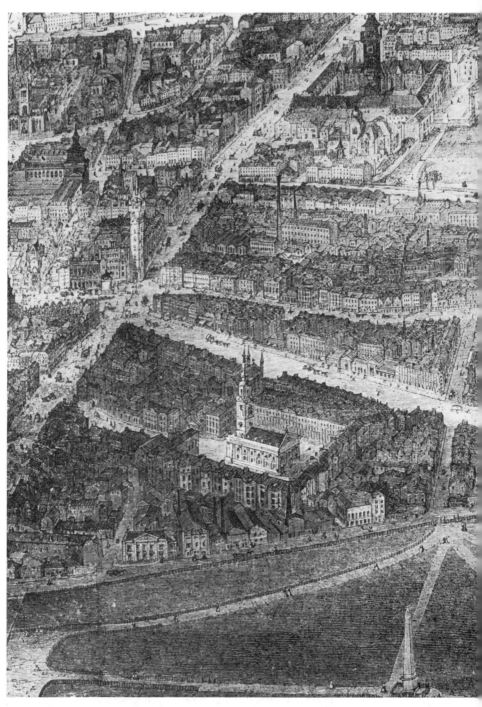

Plate 27 St Andrew's Square and the surrounding area, *c* 1860. This picture is a detail from Sulman's panorama of Glasgow, published as a supplement to the *Illustrated London News* in 1864. The bow windows of the drawing-rooms of the houses on the south side of the square can be clearly seen. The overbuilding of the city-centre is very evident.

Plate 28 (*left*) The centre section of the later part of Monteith Row. Only the presence of a close betrays that this is not a row of terraced houses.

Plate 29 (*right*) 143 Orr Street, Calton—primitive industrial housing of the 1830s. Brick was commonest as a building material in the east end of the city (see page 33).

Plate 30 *(left)* A view in the Railway Village at Corkerhill.

Plate 31 *(above)* The sweeping curve of St Vincent Crescent, part of the spectacular Stobcross development of the 1850s.

Plate 32 *(below)* The advance of the tenement − Sauchiehall Street from Garnethill. The old villas and the new tenements meet in this photograph, probably taken in the 1870s.

Plate 33 The unique north corner of 'Greek' Thomson's Queen's Park Terrace (see pages 88–9).

Plate 34 Walmer Crescent, Paisley Road West (see pages 89–90). In his simple massing of differing elements 'Greek' Thomson reveals himself as the master designer of the Victorian age.

Plate 36 Hillhead: tenements of the 1890s in Hillhead Street.

Plate 37 *(top)* Bow windows of the 1890s in Clarkston Road, Cathcart. Red sandstone tenements such as these have obviously provided the inspiration for the Woodside buildings shown in Plate 49.

Plate 38 *(above)* The Italian palazzo front of Peel Terrace, Garnethill.

Plate 39 A view in Cowlairs Railway Village. This development was the work of the Edinburgh and Glasgow Railway Company, who erected it for their employees in 1863.

Plate 40   Charing Cross, 1901. The impressive frontage of Charing Cross Mansions can be seen in the background, behind the Grand Hotel.

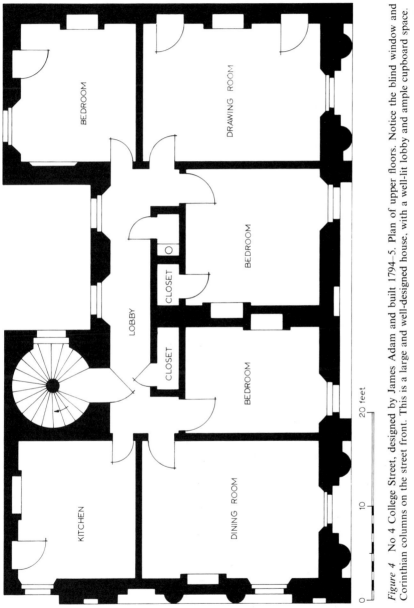

Figure 4 No 4 College Street, designed by James Adam and built 1794–5. Plan of upper floors. Notice the blind window and Corinthian columns on the street front. This is a large and well-designed house, with a well-lit lobby and ample cupboard space.

7

1800—1861

Glasgow in 1800 was a very different place from the small homely town of a century before, with fifteen small ships to carry on its trade. The population was now around 80 000, the tobacco trade had come and gone and the Industrial Revolution was in full swing, with the rapid expansion which followed inevitably in its wake.[1] It was an age of invention, of experiment, and the golden age of the speculator. The urgent need for housing was tackled by landlords, builders and architects in new ways, endeavouring to provide comfort and elegance within a practical and economical framework. It follows that during this period there was a far greater variety of plan and elevation than was possible before or since.

As we saw in the previous chapter, the main trend of city expansion was westward, but the first few decades of the new century saw developments taking place also south of the river. This district was the old Barony of the Gorbals which by this time had been divided into three distinct estates, called after their respective proprietors — Tradeston, the property of the Trades House; Hutchesontown, belonging to the Patrons of Hutchesons' Hospital; and Laurieston, which had been feued from the Hospital by James Laurie.

The Trades House decided to feu its ground west of Eglinton Street in 1790, and a plan was drawn up by John Gardner, a land-surveyor, who laid out the area with streets on a grid plan.[2] Feuing began, at the price of 1s 6d per square yard, the following year, and the first house was built in Centre Street. Demand was brisk, and by 1798 James Denholm could write:

> The principal streets extend westward from the bridge, and parallel with the river. Several of these are already built in a handsome stile with small courts or areas behind; and when completed, we have no scruple in saying, that it will certainly be the finest village in Scotland, whether we regard the position of its streets, its buildings, or the very healthful and pleasant situation in which it is situated.[3]

The streets were originally named after the fourteen Incorporated Trades, but for some reason were soon changed; Skinners Street becoming Commerce Street; Convener Street becoming Centre Street; and Fleshers Street, Cook Street.[4]

With the rapid spread of the city, Tradeston quickly lost its village atmosphere. By mid-century, domestic architecture was giving way to industrial, and large areas had already been taken over for the Johnstone canal and the Greenock railway. Eventually even the Green or public park along the riverbank gave way to warehouses. Being such a mixed development, the district was quickly built over, and as early as the 1850s redevelopment had begun, with the result that today few of the original buildings remain.[5]

There was little attempt to control the appearance of the buildings in the new suburb. Conformity to an approved elevation was not imposed, with the result that the total effect has always been one of fairly haphazard development. The earliest tenements were two or three stories in height, the latter usually having projecting stair-towers at the rear. The corners were never curved, but were enhanced with moulded gable-pediments.

Also along the south bank of the river, and immediately east of the old village of the Gorbals, was the contemporary suburb of Hutchesontown. The plan there also was in the form of a grid, but with the chief frontages facing east and west. The first building was erected in St Ninian Street in 1794.[6] The Hospital, from the beginning, exercised much greater control than the Trades House. As early as 1790, the minimum width of streets was fixed at 70 feet, including 10-foot pavements on each side, and the width of lanes was fixed at 30 feet. The main north–south thoroughfare, Hospital Street, was to have the greatest width of all.[7]

The street frontages also appeared much more orderly than those of Tradeston, a uniform height of four stories having been adopted almost from the outset. Eventually Crown Street became the main thoroughfare because of its alignment with the south end of the Saltmarket on the other side of the river, to which it was later joined by the Albert Bridge. It was Crown Street also which was linked to the main road southwards, and in which the Hospital erected its new school in 1839–41.

Hutchesontown began as a middle-class development, but by mid-century, with the growth of a multiplicity of industries close by, it subtly changed to a working-class area. This change, however, was not obvious from external evidence. The front elevations of the tenements remained uniform, with moulded surrounds to the upper windows and each block continuous with the next, forming an almost unbroken pattern. Internally, the arrangements tended to be superior, with much greater attention to sanitation than one usually found. The best houses were in Hospital Street, which was divided into sections with the names Walmer, Bryce, Castlemilk and Lucknow Place. The houses were of three, four or five apartments, usually arranged two on a landing.[8]

Laurieston, occupying the area between Gorbals village and Tradeston, began to be developed in 1800, a little later than the two districts already described. The proprietor, James Laurie, was, according to tradition, well-known in London circles and on friendly terms with many of the southern nobility, after whom he named the streets of his new suburb — Norfolk, Oxford, Warwick, Sussex, Portland etc. The main street was called Laurie Street, but as early as the 1830s it had been renamed Abbotsford Place. The plan and scale of this new suburb were much more ambitious than in either of the two earlier schemes, and the overall control much greater.

> To Builders and others. Eligible building ground in Laurieston, presently feuing off by private bargain. A variety of principal steadings all fronting elegant streets of from 60 to 80 ft broad. Few situations possess equal advantages. The foundation is dry, consisting of sand and gravel: in the immediate vicinity of the banks of the river and of several important improvements; surrounded by property laid out according to an extensive and elegant plan: all under every necessary restriction in regard to nuisances: and though not 9 minutes walk from the Exchange, the situation is pleasant, healthful, genteel, and most agreeable for places of residence.[9]

A grid plan was adopted in the same manner as in Hutchesontown, with the main frontages facing east and west. The scheme began with the erection of two terraces in Carlton Place, facing the river — the first example of a true terrace in the city. They are plain structures, unremarkable on the exterior, but with some very fine plasterwork in the central houses of the eastern block.[10] James Laurie commissioned that versatile architect Peter Nicholson to design the whole scheme, and it is now his only work remaining in Glasgow.

After the completion of Carlton Place, building spread gradually southward, until by the end of the period the whole area had been built over. The main arteries were South Portland Street with Abbotsford Place, and Bridge Street with Eglinton Street (originally called Bloomsbury and Marlborough Street). The houses were almost without exception in four-story tenement blocks and intended for middle-class families. They were large, generally of five to seven apartments, with all modern conveniences except a bath. Most of the feus were large enough to accommodate double tenements, thus allowing two large houses on each flat.

A typical tenement was No 10 South Portland Street, built in the early 1820s and demolished in 1970. It was of four stories with two houses of seven apartments on each floor. The front elevation had eight windows on each of the upper floors, lighting the front rooms of each house. A central close led to the stair, which rose at the back of the building and was lit by windows in the rear wall. There was a continuous curved flight from landing to landing. The lobbies ran lengthwise in the centre of the building with a wc at the inner end. The kitchens flanked the stair well, each with its bed-recess for a servant, and beyond were two bedrooms. At the front, a dining-room and drawing-room flanked a small bedroom. Each floor, at the time of demolition, had been subdivided into six houses, two of three and four of two apartments.

The finest part of this street, however, was Abbotsford Place. The earliest range, Nos 1–47 on the east side, was built between 1831 and 1836 and, being completed to the original design, formed one of the few examples of a unified frontage in the city. All the tenements were double and four stories in height. The street elevation had a rusticated ground floor, pierced at regular intervals by the porches of the street houses, which had Classical columns and entablature. Between each second pair was the close entrance, treated simply as an opening, which led straight through the building and gave access to the two stair-towers. Each of the upper floors was occupied by a single house of six apartments — dining-room, drawing-room, three bedrooms, kitchen and wc, all entered from the central lobby. The front and back elevations of Abbotsford Place were among the most impressive

FRONT ELEVATION

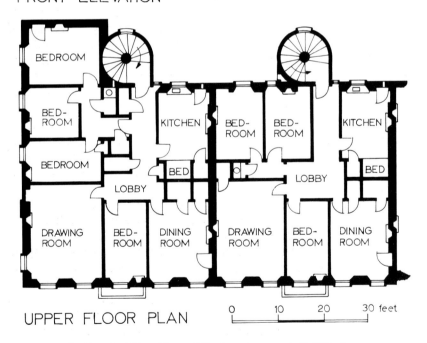

UPPER FLOOR PLAN

0   10   20   30 feet

Figure 5   1–5 Abbotsford Place. Fine middle-class tenements built 1831–6.

architectural achievements in Glasgow, and their demolition was one of those senseless acts of vandalism for which the city has become notorious.

Buildings in the other streets tended to be plainer and less ambitious. A typical early example was No 37 Eglinton Street, a three-storied, ashlar-fronted building with a projecting brick stair-tower at the back, reached by a central close. The upper flats were divided into two houses, each of three apartments, with a small wc. The later tenements continued to be of superior quality with particularly good street elevations, giving an aristocratic air to the entire scheme. In recent years the area has been the subject of comprehensive redevelopment and today, apart from Carlton Place, only a few buildings remain.

North of the river, and eastward from the earlier development at St Andrew's Square, the city magistrates had the idea of building a range of superior houses overlooking Glasgow Green. This took some time to gestate, but in 1812 the eminent architect David Hamilton was commissioned to draw up plans for these Calton Green buildings.[11] Building was slow, for David Smith's map of the city (1821) shows only two tenements standing at the west end of what was later to be known as Monteith Row. From the outset a unified frontage was intended, and to that end it was made compulsory to use David Hamilton's elevation. That being so, it comes as a surprise to find that after the first three buildings, the elevation was changed. The early part had been of four stories and typical of good tenements in other parts of the town, but the new one, of three stories, attic and basement, had the appearance of a terrace rather than of tenements (Plate 28). That this was a conscious delusion is borne out by the plans, where every effort was made to disguise or hide the close and stairs in order that in elevation each block might appear as a single house. It was only at the back that the true nature of the buildings was revealed.

Behind the contrived frontages was a surprising variety of plans. Some tenements were single, some double, and in at least two examples even triple, entry to the third being effected from the staircase of one of the other sections of the building. A typical layout had a ground-floor house with a separate entrance to the street, five apartments on that level and three more, including the kitchen, in the basement.[12] A similar arrangement was found in the top flat, which had five apartments on the top floor and three more in the attic. The first-floor houses had five apartments only, but had the advantage of being in the most favourable situation. It is interesting to note that a chimney-sweep's small boy stuck in a vent in Monteith Row in 1840, before the Chimney-Sweepers' Act forbidding the use of children for sweeping was extended to Scotland.[13]

Monteith Row was such a success that the magistrates obtained an Act of Parliament to open up a new street leading directly to it from the Cross. This was called London Street, and the foundation of the first building, on the corner of the Saltmarket, was laid with great pomp and ceremony on 30 April 1824. The plans for both the street and the buildings were by the Glasgow architect John Weir. The street was to be 70 feet wide, and the buildings of uniform design. Unfortunately, railway operations during the last century have played havoc with the section of the street that was completed, and today only two mutilated fragments survive.

The elevations were of four stories, with massive pilasters linking first and second floors, and central pediments to each block, as at Monteith Row. The cost of the scheme was enormous even for those days, and a joint-stock company was formed to finance it.

> At the time when London Street was projected it was illegal to sell property by way of public lottery, but the directors ... got over this difficulty by making it a private drawing of chances among the subscribers themselves. In Parliament this was considered an evasion of the Lottery Act, and the directors were threatened with an action for transgressing the law; but as the improvement was represented as being so beneficial, so important for the city of Glasgow, the members ... who denounced the scheme ... were induced to withdraw their opposition.[14]

Apart from new projects such as these, much rebuilding of old properties took place during this period. One interesting example stands at the southwest corner of Sauchiehall Street and Buchanan Street. It is known as the Cleland Testimonial, having been erected as a public tribute to the statistician, historian and Superintendent of Public Works, James Cleland, in 1834–5. It actually consists of two tenements, but it is the corner one which is outstanding, with its fine, curved corner-feature, which appears internally as a circular parlour. The original houses had four or five spacious apartments and were provided with internal sanitation. The architect was David Hamilton.[15]

The examples of tenements and developments so far described have all been for the more wealthy section of the population. Working-class dwellings from the early part of the century have not usually survived the passage of time and changes in standards. A few, however, did survive until recently in the eastern part of the old burgh of the Calton, in Orr Street, a thoroughfare which runs north from Bridgeton Cross. At No 162 there was a group of six three-story brick tenements known as Thomson's Buildings, dated 1832. They were built in two ranges of three, one behind the other and about 38 feet apart; but as each had a projecting stair-tower, at places there was

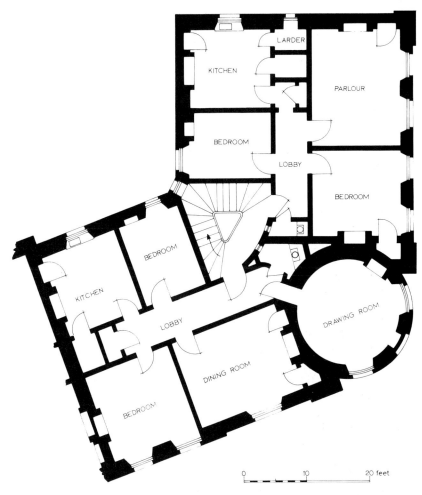

Figure 6   The Cleland Testimonial, Buchanan Street and Sauchiehall Street, 1834–5. Upper floor plan. The wc in the larger house has obviously been fitted into the awkward space which was useless for any other purpose.

only about 18 feet between them. Entrance to all six was by means of a single close, and each floor contained three houses of two apartments, making a total of fifty-four. The original sanitary provision had been primitive — one, or possibly two, outside privies serving the needs of all fifty-four families.

At No 143 a contemporary double corner-tenement still stands. It is also of three stories and built entirely of brick. A close adjoining the mean gable leads to the back-court from which access is had to the upper floors by means of two stair-towers. The appearance of the back is astonishingly primitive, and were the material not brick, one would find difficulty in dating the structure (Plate 29). There were six houses of two apartments and two single-ends on each floor. Possibly the most noticeable internal feature is the lack of cupboard space, owing to the exceptionally thin walls.

In the 1840s, as has already been mentioned in Chapters 1 and 2, an effort was being made to improve conditions such as existed in the Calton. The professional journals frequently published letters and articles on the subject of improved houses for the working class. *The Builder*, with typical Victorian outlook, wrote:

> ... where there is not perfect privacy in a dwelling, proper self-respect, if it have existed, must give way: and if it have not existed, can never spring up: where the decencies of life cannot be observed, morality cannot but break down; where the structural arrangements are not calculated to promote and preserve cleanliness and order, any attempts at these will prove futile ...

Landlords, it continues, should be encouraged to provide well-designed houses for the humbler classes, thereby not only improving their immediate social condition, but giving them the incentive to study and improve their station in life. One enlightened individual however, James Lumsden, a city merchant, was already attempting some improvement. In 1848 he erected a four-story tenement containing thirty-one dwellings and quite exceptional in design:

> The houses on each floor are arranged along a wide central passage which communicates with the common staircase and is lighted by a window at each end. The houses are arranged with the view to giving their one main apartment the utmost value, by obviating as much as possible the necessity for performing any cleansing operations within it, and forming the bed-closets, opening out of the same, so that there is no occasion for the occupants creating

disorder by strewing their clothes about the room; for this purpose these closets, of which there are two in each house, as wide apart as possible, are made large enough to afford space for dressing and undressing in: each is closed with a door, but at the same time, in order that they may be ventilated, the side which is next to the main apartment stands only about 7 ft high, so that the air of the house circulates freely through them. The bed-bottoms are fixtures, and of rod-iron filled in with hooping, to prevent the propagation of insects, as well as the loss which is so great a grievance to the proprietors of small houses, from the use of the sparred bed-bottoms for firewood. Each dwelling has also a scullery opening out of the main apartment, and containing a dresser, sink, coal-box and press: and likewise a small well-aired larder in the outside

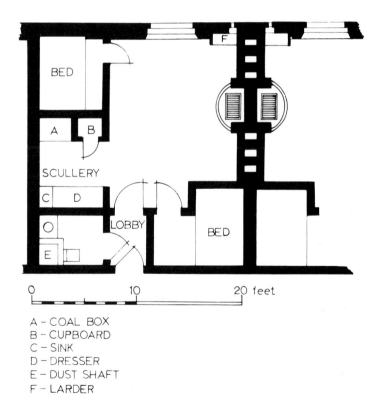

A – COAL BOX
B – CUPBOARD
C – SINK
D – DRESSER
E – DUST SHAFT
F – LARDER

Figure 7 Plan of a house in Lumsden's Model Dwellings, Dundasvale (1848).

wall: a kitchen grate with oven and boiler, an ashpit with cinder-sieve in the hearth, which is of cast iron, and includes a fender — the latter being cast with it: and opening from the small entrance-lobby, is a wc, with apparatus of simple and economical construction, with, in one corner of it, a trap covering a shoot into a dust shaft, through which all dry rubbish is conveyed to a cellar in the basement. Water is to be laid on in the scullery; and a jet of gas, for certain hours, in the main apartment, as well as in the central or common passage and staircases. The ventilation of the houses is provided for by a louvred opening in the top of each window, and of the central passages, by a few feet of the floor at either end being omitted — thus permitting a free upward circulation to the roof, where there will be large louvred outlets. There is a wash-house outside on the ground story, with all necessary appurtenances, including Robinson's rotary drying machine, which will be common to all the tenants in due succession.[16]

It will be realised from this detailed description that these were no ordinary houses. Their cost, however, was obviously a problem:

It is expected that these houses will be occupied by a superior grade of working people, as regards conduct, in whom employers may have such confidence as to become surety for their rents, and this obviates the trouble of weekly payments, and the increase of rent unavoidably accompanying that mode of collection.

The rent to be charged was £6 *per annum*, but evidently the experiment was uneconomical, for no more houses were built.

A few other developments of the 1840s deserve to be noticed. First, there was an ambitious plan for villas, terraces and tenements at St George's Cross. This was to have had two impressive blocks of tenements facing the Cross, with Corinthian porticoes modelled on Waterloo Place in Edinburgh. Only one of these was built — Clarendon Place, on the corner of Great Western Road and Maryhill Road — with some other portions of the plan. Little now remains.[17] A contemporary development, also Edinburgh inspired and consisting of mixed terraces and tenements, still survives on the other side of Great Western Road, in West Prince's Street and Queen's Crescent.

North of Sauchiehall Street, on Garnethill, feuing had begun some years earlier with the erection of a number of cottages and villas. By 1840 a more lucrative use of the land became necessary, and self-contained houses gave way to tenements (Plate 32). The first were built in Buccleuch Street, but the most impressive are those facing each other in Hill Street, on the very summit of the hill. The earlier of the two, Peel Terrace, 102–120 Hill Street, was built in 1841–2. It has a very fine Italian palazzo frontage of four stories and basement. On the south is Breadalbane Terrace, an even more elaborate range of three stories, attic and basement, erected in two sections, in 1845–6 and 1855–6. Again, the Italian palazzo is the inspiration for the street frontage, which is raised over a semi-basement. As in Monteith Row, the ground-floor houses have separate entrances, and also include the basement, while the second-floor houses include the attic. There are, however, many different features in this range. The staircase is in the centre of the building and lit by a large cupola or *lantern* in the roof. There are two houses on each flat, of six apartments with bathroom on the first floor, and of ten or eleven apartments above and below.

> Breadalbane Terrace, Hill Street. Houses to let. 8–10 apartments. These properties are very desirably situated upon rising ground on Garnethill. The drainage is perfect and the air salubrious. Rents £35 to £60.[18]

They also had their own water supply from a private reservoir on the hill.

Fired by the example of these successful schemes, yet another was begun in the West End in 1850. The *Glasgow Herald* wrote enthusiastically:

> The Stobcross lands have now been laid out with streets, terraces and crescents, underlaid with splendid common sewers, which have no connection with any other property, at an expense to the proprietors of £7000. Since the operation of forming the lands was begun, a considerable portion of the ground has been feued by a company, and shaped into a beautiful crescent. Last year, buildings to the value of more than £30,000 were erected thereon, and it is expected that an addition to nearly the same amount will be made this year. In the front of the crescent two acres, enclosed with a highly ornamental railing, have been laid out as pleasure-grounds for the tenants. The architectural style of the crescent is Italian; the height of the houses 3 stories, and they are let in flats, varying each from 10 rooms

and kitchen to 5 rooms and kitchen, with, of course, all the modern improvements. The rents of these fine middle-class dwellings range from £70 to £40. This is the first crescent erected in Glasgow, and subdivided into flats, to which the advantage of pleasure-grounds has been attached.[19]

The new tenants took exception to the name Stobcross Crescent, which had been given to the property, as insufficiently genteel, and it was altered to St Vincent Crescent, the name which it still bears.

In 1856, David Bell, a somewhat eccentric city merchant speculator, and his architect Charles Wilson, advertised another new scheme in the West End, at La Belle Place.

It is intended to commence and build forthwith, so as to be ready for occupation by Whitsunday 1857, several excellent lodgings of 6, 7, and 8 apartments, beside kitchen and suitable adjuncts. The buildings will face Kelvingrove Park and have oriel windows etc. Leases will be given for 3 or 5 years.[20]

These buildings, beside the elaborate concert hall which Bell built at the same time, are now largely occupied as offices and boast a particularly ornate Renaissance frontage.

The inclusion of oriel, or more correctly in this instance, bow windows on the front elevation is of particular interest. Wilson had already used them at the back of Breadalbane Terrace, but this seems to be the first instance of their use at the front of a tenement. Such windows also feature on the tenements erected in 1859–60 on the corner of Bath Street and Holland Street for Neilson and Carmichael, a firm of speculative builders. (See Fig 8.) The architect in this case was John Burnet. He uses dwarf columns to give a rather curious effect.

The 1850s saw the emergence of Glasgow's greatest Victorian architect, Alexander 'Greek' Thomson, who, like almost all his contemporaries, turned his attention on several occasions to tenement design. Two of the ranges he designed are of a particular merit and interest. The first is the so-called Queen's Park Terrace, 355–429 Eglinton Street, where, as at Abbotsford Place, an entire block has been completed to the original unified design.

Queen's Park Terrace was built in two sections between 1856 and 1860. Equally careful about the adequacy of internal light and the creation of an architecturally satisfying façade, Thomson has produced a front elevation of startling originality. The window-spacing has been thought out with the greatest care to give an exciting rhythmic effect, and the horizontality of the whole façade has been emphasised by linking the second-floor windows with a string-course. The north corner has been chosen for special treatment, and has a concave corner bow window rising for its full height — an idea derived from the Roman temple of Venus at Baalbek (Plate 33). Internally, a number of the houses contained Thomson's distinctive Classical plasterwork. This outstanding range of tenements was demolished in 1980.

The second range is Walmer Crescent, on Paisley Road West. This

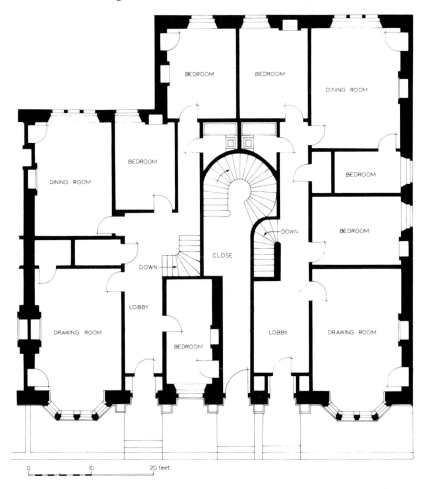

Figure 8 Ground floor plan of 246 Bath Street, a tenement of the late 1850s. The main-door houses are on two floors, and have kitchens and servants' quarters in the basement. Notice that they also have a bathroom—a luxury at this period.

is, as its name implies, a curved terrace, but only at first sight, for on closer examination it becomes apparent that it is a range of cleverly designed tenements. It has far less ornament than Queen's Park Terrace, relying for its effect on bold massing. Its severe façade is punctuated by rectangular bow windows and massive pylonic doorways, and the top floor is distinguished by a continuous collonade of windows.[21]

Even a cursory examination of the plans and elevations of the tenements described in this chapter will show how wide was the architect's scope during the first half of the nineteenth century. That many of the ideas were found to be too costly, or unsatisfactory for various reasons, is apparent in the gradual emergence of the fairly uniform plan which was to dominate design during the second half of the century.

1 J Denholm, *The History of the City of Glasgow and Suburbs*, (3rd ed 1804) pp 117 and 120–139.
2 Crawfurd, *Sketch ... of the Trades' House* p 186 gives considerable details of this scheme.
3 Denholm, *History* p 78 (2nd ed 1798).
4 'Senex', *Glasgow past and present* vol I p 63.
5 Only one of the original buildings remains at the time of writing.
6 J Cleland, *The Rise and Progress of the City of Glasgow* (1820) p 112.
7 W H Hill, *History of the Hospital and School founded ... by George & Thomas Hutcheson ...* (1881).
8 Advertisement in the *Glasgow Herald*, 6 October 1806; advertisement in the *Glasgow Constitutional*, 1 March 1837.
9 Advertisement in the *Glasgow Herald*, 3 October 1814.
10 A Gomme and D Walker, *Architecture of Glasgow* (Lund Humphries 1968) pp 72–3.
11 Marwick and Renwick, *Extracts from the Records, 1809–1922* pp 135–6.
12 Advertisement in the *Glasgow Herald*, 4 April 1851.
13 *ibid*, 10 August 1840.
14 'Senex', *Glasgow past and present* vol III p 293.
15 *Glasgow Herald*, 10 August 1835.
16 *The Builder*, 28 October 1848.
17 The plans and elevations for this ambitious project, dated 1839, were prepared by the architect Alexander Taylor.
18 Advertisement in the *Glasgow Herald*, 8 February 1856.
19 *Glasgow Herald*, 2 June 1851. See Plate 31.
20 Advertisement in the *Glasgow Herald*, 21 March 1856.
21 Gomme and Walker, pp 139–40.

8

1862–1891

If Glasgow's expansion had been great during the first half of the nineteenth century, it was completely surpassed by the vast changes of the second half. An indication may be derived from the population figures which, from 395 503 in 1861, rose to 565 839 in 1891. This increase is a reflection of the period characterised by the rise of heavy industry — the age of coal, iron and steel, with the allied industries of ship- and locomotive-building.

It was an age which also saw a change in popular housing. The middle-class areas of fifty years before were now being converted for working-class requirements, the big flats being subdivided into houses of a single or two apartments. The old residents were moving to newer schemes further from the city centre, where cottage developments after the English fashion were beginning to appear. Building houses for the working classes was to be the chief occupation of builders and speculators during the second half of the century, with the provision of new garden suburbs on the outskirts for the better-off.

Within the bounds of the old city, it was the great age of redevelopment. The activities of the City Improvement Trust in the 1860s and 70s rapidly changed the face of a number of the more picturesque, if squalid, areas of the city. The Trust demolished considerable parts of the High Street, the Saltmarket, the Calton, Bridgeton and the Gorbals, opening up what had been densely overcrowded districts. New wide streets were laid down and the standard of new buildings carefully regulated to avoid a repetition of bad conditions. It was, however, still considered desirable that working people should live close to their place of employment, and thus industrial premises were mixed with housing in the redevelopment plans. The bad effects of this are obvious. The major part of many a back-court was occupied by a factory with a chimney which, although of regulation height, belched forth smoke at all hours to the continuous discomfort of those living beside it. At the same time the Trustees, mindful of their moral obligations, rigorously forbade the use of any of their property as public houses or whisky shops.

Much criticism was levelled at landlords, builders and architects for the poor quality of many of the houses for the working class. In 1870 Dr W T Gairdner, the city's first Medical Officer of Health, complained bitterly about what he saw as defects in house construction.

> To judge by the tenements at present existing, one would say that proper means of access have literally been considered of no account by our Glasgow builders. The whole traditions of house architecture in Glasgow, the whole ideas of Glasgow builders seem to me to have been based on the principle that the mode of access to rooms was not of the slightest consequence, provided people were able to smuggle themselves into them — in fact, that the cheapest mode, the easiest mode, the darkest mode, and the dirtiest mode, was absolutely to be preferred. The usual plan of the Scotch common stair, even in the houses of the middle-classes has been all along essentially bad — a receptacle for foul air, usually closed at the top, and receiving the effluvia from all the houses on the stair, the lobbies of the individual houses being internal, and almost always unlit, except from the rooms, usually ventilating into and being lighted from, the common stair. This is the plan of thousands of houses in Glasgow, reputed fairly decent and wholesome, but which are simply a collection of sanitary abominations, and ought to be restrained and disallowed by law in newly-built houses. But when the same principle of internal lobbies or corridors, abutting upon or opening to many rooms, without separate ventilation and lighting, is carried to the tenement houses

of the poor, and especially into houses of single apartments, all the evils above indicated, with the exception of the water-closets, of which there are rarely any in such houses, are immensely exaggerated in effect and the facilities for the communication of infectious disease are correspondingly increased ... in the tenement houses of the lower working-classes it seems as if the very idea of privy accommodation had been deliberately abandoned.

In one six-story tenement

there was no water supply until quite lately: and although it is a house of 60 or 70 families, there is no water except in the close. The reason was, that the whole interior of the lobbies was so utterly dark, that to put a water supply in any lobby or landing would simply be to keep the place in a perpetual state of slop and puddle ...[1]

In their attempt to combat such problems, the Improvement Trust was continually in financial trouble. The cost of acquiring substandard property for demolition was enormous, and although the Trustees had the much criticised power to levy a percentage on the rates to finance their work, it was still continually handicapped by lack of funds. Their policy of feuing ground for development by speculative builders lasted until 1887, when they began tentatively to build for themselves, as was described in Chapter 5. The first blocks of houses were built on the east side of the Saltmarket and were designed by the Trust's architect John Carrick (see p 52). Much was made of the superiority of the plans — to the annoyance of the city's architects and builders, who found it impossible to compete. The eminent architect John Honeyman, in particular, voiced his indignation in a lecture on sanitary and social problems which he gave to the Royal Philosophical Society of Glasgow in 1888.

I have not a word to say against the buildings erected by the corporation in the Saltmarket. I agree with Dr Russell (the Medical Officer of Health) in thinking them excellent of their kind. But some of our Town Councillors seem to think that by the erection of these buildings they have done the ignorant architects and builders of Glasgow a good turn by showing them how to get up dwellings for the poor. Now that is an absurd mistake. There was no difficulty in designing or building dwellings quite equal to these in every respect, but the plain fact is that no sane builder would do anything so foolish, even if he were in the lucky position of being able to borrow money at $3\frac{1}{2}$ per cent.

He goes on to complain that the buildings are not dwellings for the poor at all, but simply an expensive tenement property to be occupied by those respectable and industrious members of the working class who can afford to do so, while the really poor are left uncared-for.[2]

Dr James B Russell, Dr Gairdner's successor as Medical Officer,

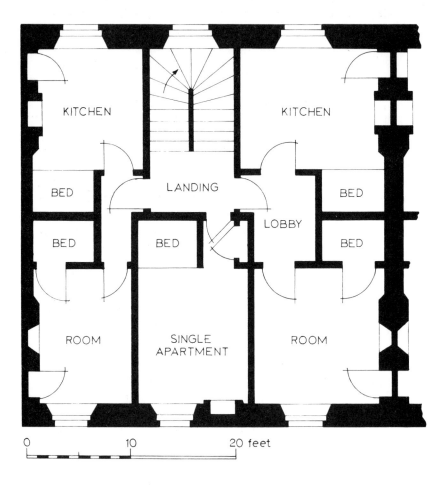

Figure 9 Upper floor plan of a typical Victorian working-class tenement. There was no internal sanitation in this example.

was equally vociferous as he waged battle against overcrowding.

> ... almost without exception these ticketed houses are what we call 'made-down houses'. No plans of these houses were ever submitted to the Dean of Guild Court. They may be either, as in the older parts of the city, in tenements erected long before the Police Act of 1866, for the gentry of old Glasgow, or in tenements which have passed the court recently as houses of 5, 8 or 10 rooms. In short, these houses have all been parts of houses of larger size; often parts of single rooms of houses of larger size, divided by partitions sometimes of mere wood, run across the floor of those large rooms. This means defective ventilation, defective light, dark lobbies, crowded stairs, and disproportion in the conveniences provided.[3]

Despite Dr Russell's criticisms, more attention *was* being paid to the matters of lighting and ventilation, water supply and sanitation. The plan of the working-class tenement was modelled on the middle-class ones of earlier in the century. It was generally four stories in height, often with shops on the ground floor, and a central close leading to the stair, which rose against the rear wall of the building, from which it was lit. On each landing were three houses, two of Room-and-kitchen flanking a single-end. There were variations on this plan according to site and area. Instead of a 2-1-2 division, it might be 3-2-3, which, if that failed to attract, could easily be subdivided to form a 2-1-2-1-2 plan. Certain districts, for example the London Road–Barrowfield area in the East End, favoured a larger number of single-apartments than would be expected in, say, the neighbouring district of Dalmarnock. Here is an example of an advertisement of good working-class property:

> TO BE SOLD. THOSE TWO NEW and SUBSTANTIAL TENEMENTS of Four Storeys, containing a shop and Houses of Two, Three and Four Apartments, forming nos. 9, 11, and 13, Watt Street, Kinning Park, fitted with all modern conveniences, and finished in a superior style, each house having Venetian Blinds and complete Bellhangings. Rental £321. Low Upset Price £3000.[4]

Working-class houses may be considered to comprise those with no more than three apartments, and it is interesting to compare the numbers of such houses built within the city proper during the period 1862–1891.

Date	1 apart	2 apart	3 apart	Total
Sept 1862–Dec 1866	602	1816	462	2880
Jan 1867–Dec 1871	3192	6889	2663	12774
Jan 1872–Dec 1876	5331	11202	4519	21052
Sept 1877–Dec 1881	1286	3344	1128	5758
Jan 1882–Dec 1886	443	1789	1053	3285
Jan 1887–Dec 1891	1153	3550	1414	6117[5]

From this, one can see that a great building boom took place in the late 1860s and up to the collapse of the City Bank in 1878. The industry did not recover until the mid 1880s when another period of prosperity began.

From 1870 the *Glasgow Herald* published a series of articles describing new building schemes in different parts of the city, and giving some idea of the extent of work then being undertaken.

During the last few years the north side of Garnethill has undergone a great transformation. Green parks, where cattle grazed, and greens where housewives bleached their clothes have been almost covered with houses — particularly in the line of West Graham Street. ... the church of Saint George's in the Fields ... is now surrounded by blocks of dwelling houses, and is therefore 'in the fields' no longer. In this district, towards the head of Saint George's Road, there has been much building of late, most of the tenements being designed for workmen's houses. ... during the past season, in this north-west district, there have been, or are about to be erected 1,069 separate dwelling houses, about 800 of which are suitable for working men.[6]

In Dorset, Belgrave, Elderslie, Pembroke and Breadalbane Streets ... we were agreeably surprised lately to find a number of fine-looking tenements nearly completed, and laid out as follows viz — 105 houses of 3 apartments each, 136 of two apartments each, and 18 of single apartments. This has hitherto been considered a middle-class part of the city, and when we find so many suitable houses for working men in course of erection at the same time and place, we cannot help regarding it as a hopeful element of progress. At the corner of St Vincent and Belgrave Streets, Mr John Robertson, coachbuilder, has just completed a first-class tenement of the same kind of houses, and intends to erect a number more; but there are no single apartments. They are all of one and two rooms and kitchen, well lighted and well

ventilated, with carriage-showrooms and shops underneath; but then the rents in the locality are high. The room
and kitchen houses in this property were all let before the
houses were habitable, at £12 per annum, and the houses of
3 apartments at £18 per annum.[7]

Further north-west, in the Hopehill–Springbank area,

Houses of two apartments ... were the rule, and either 3 or
one the exception. We met with none of 4 apartments and
in all probability none will be erected in the locality. ... We
inspected a number of new houses and found them
unexceptional, but there was one land, finished some time
ago, and fully tenanted, which tickled our fancy not a little.
It is a large four storey erection, and consists altogether of
single apartments, if we except an occasional bed-closet or
recess. There is a sunk area but it is level with the ground at
the back, and at every stair landing, there is a square
opening in the wall, considerably wider than a church
door, and fitted with an iron railing instead of glass.
Looked at from a distance, therefore, the 'land' reminds
one of a mammoth caravan for wild animals ...[8]

In the eastern districts of the city, there were being built 168 houses
of one, 409 of two, 83 of three, 14 of four and 8 of five to seven
apartments, totalling 682 new houses — and this excluding the
Improvement Trust's rebuilding of Bridgeton Cross.

Whole streets of dwelling-houses have been erected within
the past few years in this locality — one firm alone, the
Messrs Kyle of Marquis Street — having put up no fewer
than 30 tenements, each containing on an average 16
different houses. Still, however, the supply is insufficient to
meet the requirements of the increasing population.[9]

Within the city as a whole, the writer reports that during 1870 the
Dean of Guild Court had passed applications for 794 single-
apartment houses, 2052 houses of two apartments and 686 houses of
three apartments, giving accommodation for 15 000 individuals.[10] It
would seem from these figures that the author envisaged occupancy
of each apartment by two, or even three persons. However, as an
illustration of the facts of the situation, let us return to Dr Russell. He
reported a bad case of overcrowding where, in a two-apartment
house, sixteen people lived, two of whom were children under eight
and counted as one adult.

In the kitchen slept the parents and two younger children — 3 adults to 1140 cu ft or 380 cu ft each. In the parlour slept all the males — 7 adults to 1260 cu ft or 180 each. In a little room off the parlour, without a fireplace, slept all the females — 5 adults to 580 cu ft (the room was 9 ft by 6 ft 6 in, and 10 ft high) or 116 each. Of the 4 sleeping in the kitchen, two were seized with typhus: of the 7 in the parlour, 3: and of the 5 in the closet, 4. Of the inmates, 3 were nephews and a niece, and one was a young man, a lodger, but even if the inmates had been restricted to the family of the householder, there would still have been only 270 cu ft per inmate. The rent of the house was £9 10/–. The wages of the householder, an engineer, were 28/– per week; a girl was employed at 11/– per week, two boys at 8/– and 4/– each per week, and the lodger made 17/– per week.[11]

There is no lack of house room in Glasgow, he continued; the real difficulty would seem to be to get people to utilise it.

The proposal ... of the corporation to build extensive blocks of artizans' dwellings can scarcely be called reasonable if it but tends to depreciate existing house property without a cause.

Certainly, families such as were described above would not benefit by such erections, unless placed under proper supervision. Dr Russell obviously agreed with John Honeyman and the rest of the architectural profession in Glasgow.

One of the most interesting phenomena of the second half of the century was the growth of the small burghs on the city's edge. Most of these had taken advantage of the Police Acts of 1850 and 1862, which allowed 'populous places' of 1200, or later, 700 inhabitants to become independent Police Burghs. This, of course, enabled them to frame by-laws and to set up their own Dean of Guild Courts to supervise the erection of new buildings.[12]

The first of these new communities was in the west, at Partick, including Partickhill and Whiteinch, which obtained burghal status in 1852 with a population of over 5000. This rapidly increased to 10 917 by 1861 and to 17 693 in 1871, due largely to the erection of shipyards and other industries along the rivers Clyde and Kelvin. The character of the place changed equally rapidly. The old village of crow-stepped cottages disappeared, to be replaced by working-class tenements while, as building spread northward along Byres Road, an area of middle-class tenements grew up beside the new university. Partickhill, one of the early garden suburbs developed since the late 1830s with villas and cottages, now changed to an area of middle-class tenements. Whiteinch, on the other hand, was always a working-class district which grew up beside the attractive new Victoria Park (opened 1887). Partick survived as an independent burgh until 1912.[13]

The second of these burghs was Maryhill, in the north-west, formed in 1856 and absorbed into the city in 1891. It traced its origin to the construction of a dock on the line of the Forth and Clyde canal, which was opened for navigation to this point in 1775. Along the line of the canal, industries sprang up during the thirty-five years of independence, and most of the surrounding area was quickly filled up with houses for their workers. Maryhill, however, was the largest of the suburban burghs and stretched southward along the river Kelvin, where middle-class terraces and tenements were built in the 1860s and 70s as an extension of the Kelvinside estate on the other side of the river. The typical Maryhill tenement, along Maryhill Road or Kelvinside Avenue, consisted mainly of two-apartment houses with an occasional single-end, and had three or four houses on each floor. Internal sanitation was usually provided, if only communally on the half-landing. By the 1890s, almost the whole area was built over.[14]

Govan, on the south bank of the Clyde, was a village going back further in history than any of the others. By 1864, however, when it became a burgh, its character was changing fast. The picturesque eighteenth-century cottages of the rural village, so lovingly sketched by T C F Brotchie, were fast disappearing before expanding shipyards and docks.[15] Govan burgh included part of Ibrox and Bellahouston to the south, as well as stretching eastward far enough to include Plantation. The population in 1864 was 9058, but it had doubled by 1871 and in 1891 stood at 62 911, making the burgh one of the most densely populated in Scotland. With Partick, it fought bitterly for its freedom in 1891, when Glasgow sought to annex all the surrounding burghs, and, like its neighbour across the river, retained independence until 1912.[16]

Govan was chiefly a working-man's burgh, though like Maryhill it had its middle-class areas on the southern boundary, particularly along Paisley Road West. The standard of housing generally was superior to that found in many other districts. Houses of two apartments predominated, with a few single-ends, and wcs were usually provided within the building. Figure 10 illustrates, as an example, a tenement in Golspie Street, built in 1878. The front elevation is impressive, clearly influenced by 'Greek' Thomson, and has a surprising amount of window space. There are no fewer than four three-light windows on each of the upper floors.

The advantage of living in one of these new burghs was that one did not have to pay the higher city taxes, and this certainly enhanced their popularity. By 1872, building in Govan was brisk:

> Plantation is now in course of becoming an additional suburb. ... Its green fields are now intersected by numerous streets, and dwelling houses are starting up on every side.[17]

Most of these houses were of two or three rooms and kitchen. At the same time, thirty tenements, capable of accommodating about five hundred families, were being built in the centre of the burgh.

In the south, in Clifford and Percy Streets, around the new Bellahouston Academy (1876), tenements containing houses of four and five apartments, with bow windows, were being built. A rather fine example can be seen a short distance to the north-east, on the east corner of Paisley Road West and Harvie Street. The frontage is in French Renaissance style with a corner turret, and dates from 1881. Above the ground-floor shops are one house of four and one of five apartments, both with bathrooms, on each flat.

The fourth burgh, Hillhead, grew along the line of the new Great Western Road, and was formed in 1869. Starting in the early part of the century as a garden suburb, it changed about mid-century from villas to terraces and tenements of a very high class indeed.

> TO LET 1 Granby Terrace, Hillhead. A magnificent FLAT of Ten Apartments, fitted up with Kitchen Range supplying Hot Water, Bath, Washhand Basins, Pantry, Jawbox, etc.[18]

Hillhead was a small community — occupying only 131 acres — and thus was extremely vulnerable to Glasgow's annexation plans, succumbing to the first successful one in 1891, after an existence of only twenty-two years. Being so limited in size, it was soon built over, this being accomplished by the end of the century. The standard of housing, however, did not deteriorate. A range of tenements in Hillhead Street, erected as late as 1891 – 2, still had houses of four and five large apartments with bow windows in each dining-room. Because of the high standard of its buildings, Hillhead remained almost unchanged until after the second World War, when Glasgow University began to redevelop its property in the area.[19]

The Burgh of Kinning Park existed from 1871 to 1905.[20] A small

Figure 10   A tenement in Golspie Street, Govan, of 1878. Front elevation. The influence of 'Greek' Thomson can be clearly seen in the treatment of the windows as external ornaments on the wall-surface as well as necessary parts of the plan.

industrial community sandwiched between Govan and the city, it grew up almost entirely in the 1870s and 80s. Factories and houses were intermingled to a much greater extent than in any other district. There were no open spaces except those provided by railway and goods yards, although, of course, one could look across to the wooded gardens of Pollokshields. The houses were similar to those in Govan or Maryhill, mainly of two apartments with a few single-ends.

The smallest of the burghs was Crosshill, then on the southern edge of the city, which had an independent existence of only twenty years, from 1871 to 1891. It was purely residential, consisting of three streets containing villas, a terrace and a number of blocks of middle-class tenements around the Victoria Road entrance to the Queen's Park. Those along Queen's Drive were mostly built during the 1870s and include some good examples of their kind. Royal Crescent, Nos 44–74 (already referred to in Chapter 3), makes bold use of bow windows on its curved frontage. Number 148 is an exceptionally large tenement with no less than seven single-light windows flanked by bows. Its fine staircase has already been noted. Number 154, on the other hand, is much smaller than its neighbour, but has its upper windows carefully treated to form an attractive central feature.

The most spectacular of the tenements is the range formerly known as Balmoral Crescent, 80–116 Queen's Drive, erected in 1884–6. Its erection was a matter of interest to the Burgh Dean of Guild Court, for it was alleged that alterations had been made to the plans without approval. Building was allowed to continue, however, but a close look will reveal some odd features, including sculptured heads of the architect and builder looking distinctly ridiculous among the caryatids.

The history of the suburb of Pollokshields illustrates the strength of class snobbery at this period — when the Empire was at its height. Instead of becoming a single decent-sized burgh, it split into two, the boundary being the centre line of Shields Road. To the west was Pollokshields Burgh, an exclusive villa development, and on the other side East Pollokshields, an area of middle-class tenements. Both burghs were on the Nether Pollok estate and were strictly controlled by the superior, who would not allow tenements higher than three stories. This, coupled with wide streets, and a number of open spaces, has ensured that the area remained attractive. A typical house advertisement reads:

> House of Five Apartments at present To Let, 6 Doon
> Terrace, Pollokshields, in excellent condition, newly
> painted and papered by an intending tenant: annual rent
> £28: nominal rent till Whitsunday, free of City Taxes.[21]

East Pollokshields was the shortest-lived of the suburban burghs,
existing for only twelve years, from 1879 to 1891.

North of Crosshill and interlinked with it was the burgh of Govanhill,
formed in 1877 and also annexed in 1891. A working-class burgh, it
housed the employees of Dixon's Govan Ironworks, and the Queen's
Park Locomotive Works. Dixon was the superior, and when the
district was laid out in the 1870s he ensured wide streets and a good
standard of housing throughout the development. The houses ranged
from two to four apartments, almost all with internal wcs to the
individual houses and with a fair proportion of bathrooms.

One other small burgh remains to be mentioned — Pollokshaws,
about three miles south of the city centre, formed as a Burgh of
Barony in 1812, and as a Police Burgh in 1858. Being further from the
city than the others, it managed to escape annexation until 1912.
Despite its country setting, it was really an industrial community, for
the water power provided by the White Cart had been an attraction
since the mid-eighteenth century. Surrounded by bleachfields,
printfields and tanneries, the village managed to retain its distinctive
atmosphere until Glasgow's redevelopment plan of 1958 destroyed
the last traces of its individual existence.[22]

North of the river, tenement building in the country districts of
Parkhead, Shettleston and Tollcross, now within the eastern limits of
the city, was largely confined to two-storied buildings with an outside
stair, and was really rural in type. Springburn, on the main road to the
north-east, began in similar fashion, but by mid-century it had
become an important railway centre. In 1863 the Edinburgh and
Glasgow Railway Company held a competition for the design of a
model village at their Cowlairs Locomotive Works, to be built on the
hillside above. It was won by Andrew Heiton of Perth, an architect
already well-known in railway circles.

> The site of this new town is immediately to the south of the
> Cowlairs Station. The sloping nature of the ground admits
> of the series of blocks of houses being built in the form of
> terraces or crescents, and these blocks it may be observed

are in four different styles of architecture. Each house will have from two to six apartments, and the rents will range from £4 to £12. In the centre of the ground is a large square with a water fountain in the middle: and to give picturesque effect to the whole, at the corners of the square are shops, with pointed slate roofs, for a baker, butcher, grocer, and a dairy. The buildings also include a schoolhouse and library in the Tudor style, together with recreation grounds for workmen and their families. The outlay by the Railway Company for the buildings etc., is estimated at about £30 000.[23]

In the end the project proved too ambitious for the railway company who, after building four blocks of tenements, abandoned the scheme. The portion of the village which was built, however, remained one of the sights on the Edinburgh to Glasgow route until its demolition in the 1970s (Plate 39).

On the south side of the city, the district of Mount Florida was annexed, like Springburn, in 1891. By that time, however, it was already a well-developed area, mainly of middle-class tenements similar to Crosshill. The fine range of tenements along the north side of Stanmore Road and the spectacular blocks of Hampden Terrace climbing the steep slopes of Prospecthill Road date from the 1870s. These steep hill slopes of Mount Florida have given rise to some interesting and attractive features. Some of the entrances of Hampden Terrace, for example, are approached by most unusual curved double staircases. The same feature occurs on the east side of Brownlie Street (formerly Randolph Terrace) where the architect has been able to fit a second close leading to the ground-floor houses underneath the main entrance.

Further south, the old village of Cathcart was taken into the city in 1912. By that time it was really a dormitory suburb, but had managed to retain a character of its own despite the gradual encroachment of the city. The housing was mixed and somewhat haphazard. One particularly good tenement deserves special mention, as it was considerably advanced for its period. This is Lindsay Buildings, 38 Snuff Mill Road, built in 1863–4 and designed by John Baird II. It has three stories and basement, and is in Scottish Renaissance style, with crow-stepped gables etc. It stands on a most attractive site on the bank of the White Cart beside the old bridge and mill of Cathcart, for the owner of which it was built. The stair rises just inside the close door at the street front of the building, and the main rooms, one with a bow window, overlook the river on the other side. There are two houses of four apartments, with an internal wc, on each upper floor. One larger house occupies half of the ground floor and half of the basement, with a porch added to the side of the building. The other half of the basement contains the communal facilities of wash-house, coal cellars etc for the other tenants.

Returning to the city, a large-scale redevelopment took place at Charing Cross at the very end of the period.[24] It consists of a large block of shops and houses, built for Robert Simpson and Sons, warehousemen, and has frontages to three streets. Begun in 1889 and completed in 1891, it has a frontage which is an elaborate study in different phases of French Renaissance, from the semi-fortified style of the Loire Valley to the sophisticated Parisian Grand Manner. The curved front has a beautifully sculptured clock, and rises to an impressive tall turret. The walls are of red sandstone, one of the earliest examples of its use in a major building in the city. Above the shops are houses of four, five and six apartments with bathrooms. There is an ingenious system of internal ventilation above the doors to all the rooms. The architects were Burnet, Son, and Campbell, the last-named partner residing himself in one of the flats. By the 1880s the term 'tenement' had already become identified with working-class housing, but this ambitious pile, built at a cost of £20 000, marked the beginning of a new phase. In an effort to raise the status of the building in the eyes (and ears) of intending tenants, the owners decided to give it the pretentious name of Charing Cross Mansions (Plate 40). Nevertheless, it may be said without too much exaggeration that with this splendid building the Glasgow tenement was about to take on a new lease of life.

1 W T Gairdner, 'Defects of house construction in Glasgow', *Proceedings of the [Royal] Philosophical Society of Glasgow (PRPSG)*, VII (1870–1) p 245. It is clear that Dr Gairdner suffered from the delusion that disease was carried by smell.
2 J Honeyman, 'Social and sanitary problems' *PRPSG*, XX (1888–9) p 25.
3 J B Russell, 'On the "Ticketed Houses" of Glasgow' *PRPSG*, XX (1888–9) p 12.
4 Advertisement in the *Glasgow Herald*, 7 May 1869.
5 Butt, 'Working-class housing' in Chapman, *History* p 71.
6 *Glasgow Herald*, 10 December 1870.
7 *ibid*, 15 December 1870.
8 *ibid*, 17 December 1870.
9 *ibid*, 30 June 1870.
10 *ibid*, 19 January 1871.
11 J B Russell, 'A case of overcrowding in Glasgow', *British Architect*, 1 January 1887.
12 *13 & 14 Vict c 33* (1850) 'An Act to make more effectual Provision for regulating the Police of Towns and Populous Places in Scotland, and for paving, draining, cleansing, lighting, and improving the same.' The Police and General Improvement (Scotland) Act 1862.

13 Marwick, *Glasgow — The Water Supply* Appendix p 69.
14 A Thomson, *Random Notes and Rambling Recollections of ... Maryhill 1750–1894* (1895).
15 T C F Brotchie, *The History of Govan* (1905, new ed 1938), has many illustrations of the old village before redevelopment.
16 Marwick, *Glasgow — The Water Supply* Appendix p 70.
17 *Glasgow Herald*, 31 December 1872.
18 Advertisement in the *Glasgow Herald*, 12 February 1869. See also Plate 52.
19 H B Morton, *A Hillhead Album* (1973) is a compilation of photographs, maps and reminiscences of the district.
20 Marwick, *Glasgow — The Water Supply* Appendix p 72.
21 Advertisement in the *Glasgow Herald*, 6 January 1869.
22 A McCallum, *Pollokshaws — Village and Burgh 1600–1912* (1925) contains a lot of information about this old community.
23 *The Builder*, 4 April 1863.
24 Gomme and Walker, pp 196 and 202.

9
1892–1918

The Burgh Police (Scotland) Act of 1892 was perhaps the most influential of the many passed in an attempt to improve living conditions. Control over the number of houses which could be provided in new tenements was something new, and has been noted in Chapter 2. The fact that twice the number could be provided if the balcony system was used meant that many more on that principle were erected. The compulsory provision of a wc in existing as well as new tenements resulted in the addition of the brick stacks to the back of buildings which have been such a familiar feature ever since.

Two other changes which occurred at the beginning of this period owed nothing, however, to legislation. The first was the appearance of red sandstone as the chief building material, replacing the white stone of the local quarries which was becoming exhausted. The red stone had to be brought by rail from quarries mainly in Ayrshire and Dumfriesshire, and this naturally added to the already rising costs of building. The second change was the appearance of bow or oriel windows in the great majority of tenements of all but the poorest class. This made a considerable difference to the lighting and size of the main rooms, and also changed the appearance of the long street vistas, which from this time onwards were to be regularly broken by this new vertical feature.

The absorption of a number of the suburban burghs into the city was an incentive for increased building activity, and it did not take long for almost all the vacant ground within the city bounds to be built over.[1] As a result, it was found necessary to spread outwards into the country districts, and developments began around Cathcart and Crossmyloof on the south, Parkhead and Shettleston on the east and Hyndland on the north-west.

The new tenements, besides being of different-coloured stone and possessing bow windows, were of a somewhat larger size than had formerly characterised dwellings for the working class. Two and three apartments were normal — no single-ends — and bathrooms were frequently provided. The plans were carefully worked out without the awkward recesses often found in earlier types. As was mentioned in Chapter 3, the central staircase, with its poor lighting from the roof, gradually disappeared except at corners where the exigencies of the site precluded a back-lit stair.

In Crosshill, the last of the vacant plots facing the Queen's Park was filled at this time, completing the range of middle-class tenements begun in 1870. Large houses of seven apartments were still the rule in this prestige area. It was, however, but one of many developments on the south side of the city, as may be gathered from this contemporary report:

> The building boom in the southern districts of the city still continues, and to all appearance is likely to continue for a considerable time to come. The openness of the localities, their freedom from smoke, and the splendid travelling facilities afforded by the Corporation cars, the omnibuses, and the Cathcart District Railway, have induced builders to put up houses for all sorts of people. . . . Mr R B Shaw is building several red sandstone tenements of 3 and 5 and 6 rooms and kitchen houses near Pollokshields West Station, and Messrs R Muir and Son [sic] are to follow with tenements on the same stretch of ground.[2] In Allison Street, Queen's Park, Mr Alexander Marshall is busy with 3 tenements, the accommodation being two and 3 rooms and kitchen, and as soon as these tenements are finished, 3 others will be commenced.
>
> In the square of ground between Bute Terrace and Wellcroft Bowling Green Mr Murray is building houses of a very superior character, and it is his intention to cover the entire ground with buildings, excepting a piece in the centre, which will be reserved for a garden. Altogether there will be 11 tenements. The main-door houses in the

tenements at present going up range in size from 7 to 12 apartments ...[3]

Gradually the old buildings at Langside are disappearing to make room for the new, and it is probable that in a short time there will be little trace of the village left. Part of the old portion is being taken away to allow of Mr Waddell putting up 5 tenements which are to be ready in November....[4]

Adjacent to the Pollokshaws Manse Mr Aitken has just completed 5 tenements of red sandstone, and is completing a sixth tenement, his intention being to build 25. ... The houses in the tenements completed are of two and 3 rooms and kitchen, with every convenience, and it is admitted by all who have inspected them that finer finished houses of the kind have not been erected on the South Side. All the houses have been let, and are to be occupied this term.[5]

Another builder advertised his fourteen new tenements at Battlefield thus:

BATTLEFIELD GARDENS, LANGSIDE.
Three minutes from Mount Florida Station: convenient to Car and adjoining Queen's Park.
TO LET MAGNIFICENT HOUSES of TWO , THREE and FOUR Rooms and Kitchen, Light Bath-Rooms, Cloak-Room and Pantry, with Hot Water throughout: Tiled Closes, Vestibule Doors, Large Pleasure Ground in centre.[6]

Somewhat less pretentious were the tenements in Allison Street and Niddrie Road, Queen's Park, advertised for sale in 1896.

Several VERY SUBSTANTIAL TENEMENTS, consisting of Dwelling-Houses of Two and Three Apartments, with Cloak-Room, Light Bath-Room, Hot and Cold Water, Tiled Closes, and all Modern Improvements.[7]

Feuing for villas had begun on the Langside estate as early as 1852, but by the end of the century such development was uneconomic, and builders changed to tenements. Eastward towards Cathcart and westward to Shawlands, the open ground was built over in the 1890s and early 1900s with good-class red sandstone tenements. Similarly, across the Clyde, Dennistoun had ceased to be an exclusive villa suburb, and had become yet another tenement area. At first the flats had been of large size, but by the end of the century continuation of this policy was quite unrealistic, and the average house became one of three apartments. In this form, the suburb spread northwards across Alexandra Parade and eastward to Kennyhill and Haghill.

One of the most striking ranges of tenements of this period was erected by Alexander Muir and Son on the corner of Terregles Avenue and Shields Road, Pollokshields. The architect, H E Clifford, clearly went to a great deal of trouble over them. They are of three stories and constructed of fine-grained white sandstone. The elevations are severe, with practically nothing in the way of mouldings or ornamentation, surprising for the age which produced such exuberant office blocks in the city centre. The houses are of four, five and six rooms and kitchen, arranged two on a landing and entered from a central stair. There are few bed-recesses, the customary one in the kitchen being expanded to form a small servant's bedroom in most cases. All the kitchens have a large pantry. The dining-rooms measure 17 feet by 15 feet and have attractive, shallow bow windows, which form a distinctive feature of the elevations.[8]

The work of the City Improvement Trust continued in the 1890s with much rebuilding in the city centre. Both sides of the Saltmarket were completely rebuilt at that time, with a particularly pretentious block on the corner of the Trongate. Despite the fact that the Trust was now also building warehouses and office blocks on some of their properties, its most important contribution, socially and architecturally, was the building of model workmen's dwellings. Between 1894 and 1897 a large development of this kind was built at Morrin Square, Townhead (Plate 43). It consists of five four-story blocks of two-apartment houses, all with internal sanitation and designed in simple Scottish domestic style. A short distance to the north, in St James's Road, a contemporary scheme provided houses for a poorer class — twelve two-apartment houses and forty-eight single-apartments, in two blocks of harled brick, costing about £10 000.[9]

Two of the best-known of the Improvement Trust's schemes are at the Bell o' the Brae on the High Street, and at the corner of Woodlands Road and St George's Road, Charing Cross. Both are in French Renaissance style and were designed by W J Boston, of Burnet and Boston. The High Street houses are of two, three and four apartments, while those at Woodlands Road are larger — three, four and five apartments, with bathrooms. The seven tenements of the latter scheme cost £36 000.[10]

As has been noted in Chapter 8, criticism was levelled at the Improvement Trust for not fulfilling their obligation to provide adequate housing for the under-privileged poorest class of the city's population. That task was taken in hand by a private body, the

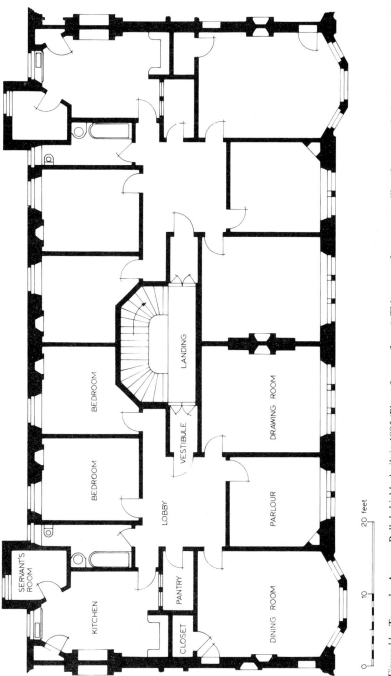

Figure 11 Terregles Avenue, Pollokshields, built in 1895 (Plan of upper floors). This range of tenements still ranks among the best and most coveted housing in Glasgow. Notice the built-in shelves in the kitchen which have taken the place traditionally occupied by the bed-recess. Despite the size and elegance of these houses, the lobbies are lit only by borrowed light from the other rooms.

111

Glasgow Workmen's Dwellings Company (see p 53), which erected, among other projects, two 'courts' of small houses in the poorer parts of the city. The first of these, Cathedral Court, was built in 1892 at a cost of around £8000.[11] That the company were mindful of more than the basic physical needs of their tenants is clear from the following contemporary account:

> The new buildings form two blocks, one towards Rottenrow and the other overlooking High St, with a courtyard about 60 ft in width and open to the east and west between them. The entrance to both blocks is obtained from Rottenrow. The north block ... is 5 storeys, and the south block ... 6 storeys in height: the two lower floors of the latter, being leased to the University Settlement Association, are to be called 'Toynbee House', after Toynbee Hall in London. They will afford ample opportunity for many forms of social intercourse between the tenants and those similarly situated, and the members of the University Settlement and allied societies. They consist on the lower floor, of a large hall, ... a drawing room, ... a kitchen, and a small library. In the drawing

BACK ELEVATION

Figure 12 St James's Road: City Improvement Trust tenements. These buildings were put up in the 1890s to house the city's poorest classes. The plan and elevation are of different tenements in the same scheme.

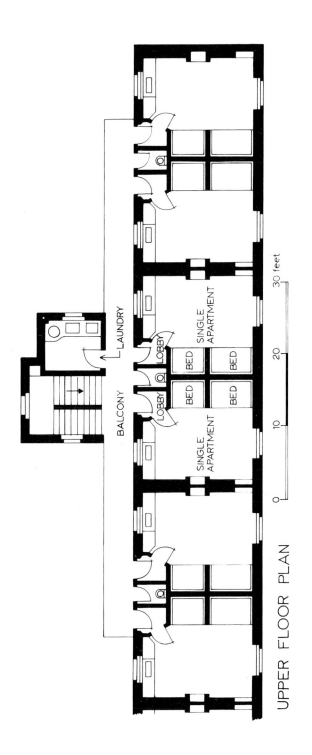

UPPER FLOOR PLAN

LAUNDRY

BALCONY

SINGLE APARTMENT

SINGLE APARTMENT

LOBBY

LOBBY

BED

BED

BED

BED

0   10   20   30 feet

113

room, evening parties will be given of a perfectly simple kind, where hosts and guests meet on the footing of friends. The hall, which will accommodate over 250 people, will be used probably twice a week as a gymnasium, and on the other nights for the meetings of the Literary Society, the singing class, and for lectures, and occasionally for smoking concerts. On the upper flat are the men's club-room with class-room attached, and the girls' club and class-rooms. . . . The remainder of the south block, and the whole of the north block are devoted to dwelling houses, 57 in all, consisting of 17 of one room, and 40 of two rooms, with a house of three rooms for the caretaker. The one-roomed houses vary in size from about 15 ft by 10 ft to about 22 ft by 10 ft, while the two-room houses consist of a living-room 14 ft by 10 ft, and a small bedroom 10 ft by 7 ft 6 in. All the rooms are 9 ft in height. The cubic capacity of the two-room houses is 1800 cu ft which at 400 cu ft per adult (the limit under the Glasgow Police Act) suffices for a family of say a man and his wife and three children under 10 years of age. . . . There is through ventilation from front to back of each house. A well-lighted and aired staircase at the east end of each block gives access to the upper floors, and balconies therefrom, facing the court, give access to the houses. The washing-houses and drying-ground are situated on the flat roofs. Water and gas are laid on to each house, and each has a kitchen range, bedroom grate, and iron bedframe. When desired by the tenant, automatic gas meters have been introduced. wc accommodation — one for every two houses — is provided on each flat, in a part of the building disconnected from the dwelling houses. A ventilated dust shaft from each flat communicates with an ash-bin on the street level. . . . The rents are meantime fixed upon a low scale ranging from 1/7¼d to 2/3½d per week for one room, and 2/5½d per week for two rooms. This rent includes water supply and cost of stair gas, but no taxes. . . . The buildings are constructed with hollow brick walls, rough-cast on the outer surface, the dressings, steps, and balconies being of red concrete. ... The floors (with the exception of the flat roof, which is of iron and concrete, finished with Limmer asphalt) are of wood. Internally the walls are plastered on the bricks without lath or straps.[12]

This development was so successful that another on a larger scale, called Greenhead Court, was erected in Bridgeton in 1897–9. This consisted of four large blocks of similar design to those already described, with crow-stepped gables, dormer windows and massive chimneys. Club and committee rooms were provided for the use of the tenants, and the courtyard contained a playshed and a row of pram-sheds. The Court was overlooked on one side by factories, but this was compensated for by the presence of a graveyard, then a well-kept open space, on the other side. Both these projects were designed by the company's architect, J J Burnet. Unfortunately, both Cathedral Court and Greenhead Court were demolished in 1971.

Much new railway-building took place in the 1890s. In 1894 the Caledonian Railway Company constructed a line from Rutherglen in the south east, through Bridgeton and the city centre below ground level, to Maryhill on the north west. The company made a special effort to promote buildings of superior quality, and to this end commissioned three private architects to design them. James Miller designed not only that much-missed Moorish extravaganza, Botanic Gardens Station, but also Kelvinbridge Station, with the range of tenements adjoining. This, called Caledonian Mansions, is a prestige building of three stories, attic and basement, with an elaborate French Renaissance frontage to Great Western Road. The top-floor flats also include the attics.

J J Burnet was the architect for some of the other stations, and also two blocks of tenements in association with them. The example at Anderston Cross has disappeared, but another still stands in the Saltmarket, near Glasgow Cross. It is a narrow block in the popular Franco-Scottish style, with houses of three apartments and bathroom on each floor above the shops.

In the east end, the North British Railway Company built five tenements in 1897–8 in connection with their new Bridgeton station. These flank the station entrance and are distinguished by corner pavilions which have massive steep-pitched roofs and finials. There are two houses to each landing, with three apartments and bathroom. The estimated cost was £15 000.[13]

The third important railway company, the Glasgow and South Western, went a stage further than its rivals. Owing to greatly increased traffic and the lack of space around the city terminus at St Enoch, they decided in 1897 to move the engine-sheds to a more open position, where expansion was possible. The site eventually chosen was at Corkerhill on the Paisley Canal line, and the company decided to build a model village for its workers beside the new sheds.

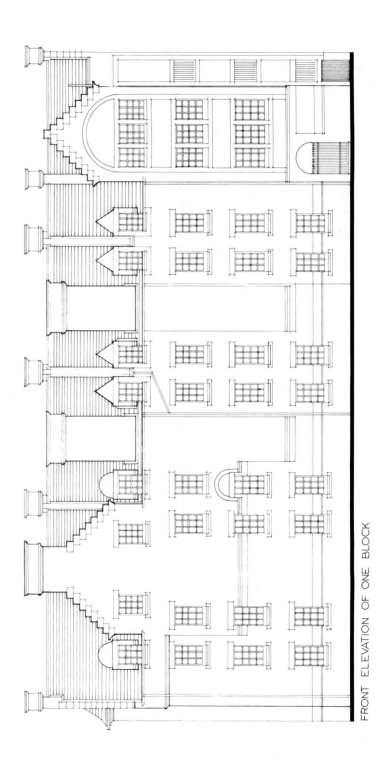

FRONT ELEVATION OF ONE BLOCK

116

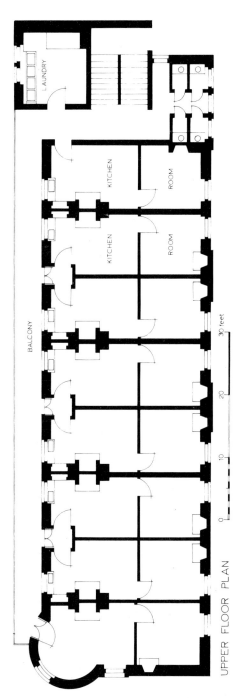

UPPER FLOOR PLAN

Figure 13 Greenhead Court, designed by J J Burnet for the Workmen's Dwellings Company (1897–9). This block contains two-apartment houses; other parts of the development had single-apartments.

117

Somewhere in the beginning of November 1897, the first of the 5 blocks of houses was tenanted, these blocks consisting of 60 dwellings, 20 of them being two rooms and kitchen houses, and 40 one room and kitchen houses. In the summer of last year [1899] other 5 blocks, consisting of 52 dwellings, were erected and ready for occupation; and these blocks contained 24 houses of one room and kitchen, 12 houses of two rooms and kitchen, and 16 houses of three rooms and kitchen. In all there were at present 112 dwelling houses at Corkerhill, and a recent census showed that the people residing there number 334 males and 268 females — in all a population of 602 souls — so that the company might boast of being the possessors of a good-sized village of their own. Although the railway company had spent a large sum of money there — in all something like £67 000 — they would require to spend still more, as the directors had in contemplation the taking in of more land, the building of more houses, and the enlargement of the engine-sheds. The directors had provided the railway institute for the double purpose of holding social and religious meetings, as well as for Sabbath Schools, Bible classes, and other services. In the hall, which was capable of holding over 300 persons, there had been provided a reading-room and library and a recreation-room, as well as a suite of baths of the most modern description, and in connection with the building, a large general store had been provided.[14]

The houses at Corkerhill, which were demolished in the 1970s like so much else of value, were arranged in two-story blocks of twelve houses each. Upper floors were reached by means of an outside stair leading to a balcony. The earlier portion had crow-stepped gables and harled brick walls, but the later part was in bright red brick. The wash-houses were particularly attractive — single-story buildings with the roof rising to a central chimney-stack.

The Art Nouveau movement was at its height at the turn of the century, but had little impact on tenement design. The important figures of Charles Rennie Mackintosh and J Gaff Gillespie did little work of that kind, and as a result very few tenements in that transitory style exist. The two most important examples were erected by banks — by the British Linen Bank in the Gorbals, and by Glasgow Savings Bank in Anderston. Both were built in 1899–1900. The

Gorbals bank is of four stories, with the bank and a shop occupying the ground floor. Each of the upper floors contains one house of three and one of four apartments. The street elevation is fairly plain, but has some distinctive sculpture and ironwork. The Anderston bank is much more elaborate. The semi-octagonal turret on the corner has some fine sculpture in low relief, but the *pièce de résistance* is undoubtedly the bank doorway with its beautiful carved figures and coloured mosaic. There are three houses of two rooms, kitchen and bathroom on each of the upper floors.[15]

The so-called Modern Movement in architecture had more influence than Art Nouveau on tenement elevations. Many examples may be seen with the typical flattened dome and distinctive mouldings. There was an interesting one in Castlebank Street, Partick, dating from 1894–5 and showing these features combined with a certain Scottish feeling.[16] Three others stand on the corner of Balgrayhill and Barclay Street, Springburn, dating from 1903.[17] Two of the finest, however, were built right at the end of the period, in 1912–13, in Rutherglen Road, Hutchesontown, by the City Improvement Trust. There were two blocks of two tenements each, designed on the balcony system, and containing houses of two apartments with wcs. The elevational treatment, as can be seen in the remaining building, is simple but effective, with a circular turret at each corner. The tenements were designed by the firm of Honeyman, Keppie and Mackintosh, and effectively brought the Trust's work to an end.

Before leaving the subject of housing for the working class, mention should be made of an experiment by Charles J Anderson, the proprietor of the well-known Argyle Street store, the Polytechnic. He purchased the old Saracen's Head Inn in the Gallowgate, built in 1755 but by the early 1900s degenerated into a slum. He decided to redevelop the site as housing for the very poor.

> The new buildings erected by Mr C J Anderson ... are now completed, and will soon be occupied by almost as many tenants as would make a decent population for a small village. On the site of the 60-stalled stable of the inn yard, there now stands a picturesque Elizabethan edifice, containing a large reading and games room for a working boys' club, a gymnasium, and baths. ... In addition there are a reading-room and a lecture-hall, where women can have some intellectual diversion after the domestic duties of the day. ... An elegant fountain, 14 feet in height, will be

erected in the centre of the yard. The yard itself will be so
arranged that tenants can sit out in chairs during summer
and enjoy the open air.[18]

On the street was the block of tenements, of a specially-chosen red
freestone, with a simple but effective elevation of French Renaissance
type. Being for the very poor there was a large proportion of single-
apartments — thirty-two in all, the rest being of two apartments.
Each landing had two communal wcs, only the single large house
(reputedly for the owner's use) having internal sanitation. There were
six baths and four wash-houses provided in the back-court. The cost
was about £10 000, and the architect T L Watson. Most of the

Figure 14 Inverclyde Gardens, Broomhill Drive, Partick. 'Baronial' extravagance of 1902.
Notice especially the highly ornamented down-pipes from the roof.

buildings were removed in 1974.

The Victorian age staged a last show of effrontery and exuberance in Broomhill Drive, Partick, where a range of tenements with a highly ornate frontage was put up in 1902. Inverclyde Gardens, as they were originally called, cannot easily be fitted into any architectural category, although the appearance of turrets and waterspouts on the skyline prompted contemporaries to refer to them as 'Baronial'! Following tradition, the ground-floor houses have separate front doors, and also include the basement, having a total of six rooms and kitchen. The upper floors have two houses of three rooms and kitchen on each floor, reached by a staircase in the centre of the building.

Much more sober elevations were the norm, however. In Fotheringay Road, Pollokshields, H E Clifford designed a second range for Alexander Muir & Sons in 1902. Unlike the earlier example in Terregles Avenue, this is of red stone, with an elevation which might be described as Modern French. The houses are large — five, six and seven apartments, with servant's room and bathroom. The effect of the corner turret at the west end is remarkably good. The cost of these luxury flats was about £34 000, or £4250 per tenement, a rise of about £600 since 1895, when those in Terregles Avenue were built.

Needless to say, the builders of working-class tenements made great efforts to sound equally grand, with somewhat comic results:

> TO BE LET. EXCELLENT ONE ROOM and KITCHEN HOUSES.
> With Light Bath-Room, Hot and Cold Water, Grate and Gasalier in Room, Lamp in Lobby, Iron Bed in Kitchen; splendid Press accommodation, Superior finish and good position adjoining Tram Lines, within 5 minutes Walk of Beardmore's Works and Carntyne Station.[19]

It seems that competition was very keen in those early years of the new century, with the market for large flats gradually diminishing; and it was found necessary to publicise all the possible benefits of any new property.

> DARNLEY ROAD AND BOLEYN ROAD, POLLOKSHIELDS, opposite Moray Place, with open Southerly exposure, Two Minutes from Pollokshields West Station.
> TO LET. SUBSTANTIAL HOUSES of 4 and 5 ROOMS and KITCHEN, One or Two Main Doors, Electric Light Fittings, all Grates, Ranges, Copper Boilers, Tanks, Closes and Staircases Tiled throughout, Terazzo Steps and Landings, and all other up-to-date improvements.[20]

TO LET. MINARD ROAD CROSSMYLOOF Nos 11 and 19 — NEW
HOUSES of TWO and THREE ROOMS and KITCHEN.
Light Bath-Room, Hot Water throughout, Ranges,
Grates, Blinds, Electric Bells, Laundry Poles. Extra Well
finished.[21]

The changes which were taking place in some of the old suburbs
were occasionally described in the local press, and give us some idea of
the opinions of those who witnessed them.

Anyone who knew Partickhill half a century ago, and who
had not seen the district since, would have some difficulty
in recognising familiar landmarks. ... the modern
tenement, with its artistic and utilitarian attractions,
threatens ere long to supplant the villas which have been its
leading feature for so long a time. ... with all its internal
conveniences, [it] is a very wonderful development of a
class of building with which Scotland has been familiar for
some centuries. The building ... known as Crown
Mansions, is situated at the corner of Partickhill Road and
North Gardner Street, ... and is part of the work being
carried out by the Partickhill Building Company. The
architect, Mr Thomas Baird jun. IA, 134, Bath Street, set
to himself the task of producing what he regards as 'ideal'
houses of the 4 and 5 rooms and kitchen class. It will be for
the public to say whether he has succeeded, but certainly
the houses in the block referred to ... strike one as being
nothing short of luxurious as compared with houses of the
same class built ten or a dozen years ago, each property
being fitted with Corporation telephones for the use of the
tenants.[22]

Close by is Hyndland, the most important of the tenement schemes
promoted in the early 1900s, and which has recently been declared a
conservation area — the first all-tenement district to be taken
seriously. There is no particular class of house in the scheme, but a
variety, containing from three to eight apartments, in well-designed
and attractive red sandstone blocks on wide streets. Building began in
1898, and the scheme was completed about 1910. It was in 1908, in an
advertisement for new flats there, that the ultimate in luxury seems to
have been achieved:

TO LET. AT YORK DRIVE. Near Kelvinside and Hyndland Car
Stations Best Amenities in Glasgow — These beautifully-
finished, High-Class new two and three Room and Kitchen

Houses. Granite columns at Entrances, Large Parlours, Sculleries, Light Bath-Rooms, Electric Light Fittings, Ranges with Tiled Surrounds, Polished Mahogany Mirrored Mantelpieces, with Art Tiled Interiors. ...[23]

But this was the end — Lloyd George's Finance Act of 1910 signalled the cessation of private tenement-building, since it made it quite uneconomical. Builders like John Mactaggart, who had been involved in the development of Hyndland, changed their house-types to bungalows and cottages, and it seemed that the age of the tenement had come to an end. Economic depression and the far-off rumblings of war in central Europe heralded the disaster which was to break out in 1914, and which was to be the worst and most unnecessary carnage in human history. On Armistice Day 1918, the crowds certainly cheered — cheers of relief — but in their hearts they must have known that life would never be the same again.

1 *54 & 55 Vict c 130*, The City of Glasgow Act 1891.
2 Terregles Avenue, Pollokshields.
3 The area in which John Murray was building was originally called Cromwell Square, now Niddrie Square.
4 Mr Waddell's tenements were in Algie Street and Langside Place.
5 William Aitken's fine tenements were in Grantley Gardens. *Evening Times*, 13 May 1895.
6 Advertisement in the *Evening Times*, 25 February 1895.
7 Advertisement in the *Glasgow Herald*, 13 January 1896.
8 POLLOKSHIELDS TO LET. Very Superior and Highly finished NEW HOUSES of 5 and 6 Rooms and Kitchen, with Servants' Bed-rooms, Pantries, and Bath Rooms, in Terregles Ave and Shields Rd, adjoining Pollokshields West Station. The 6 Room houses on Ground Floor have Main Doors. These Houses occupy the finest situation in the district, and have a most extensive country view. Apply Alex Muir and Sons, 400, Eglinton St. (*Glasgow Herald*, 20 April 1896.)
9 Kay, *The Corporation of Glasgow* pp 10–12, gives factual information on this scheme: 'The proximity of the St James' Road block to the Blind Asylum enables several houses to be let to the workers in that institution, whose wages, owing to their blindness, are even below the average wages of the unskilled labourer. The female tenants are widows, either making a living as charwomen, or supported on the earnings of their children.'
10 *ibid* pp 44–45. Both schemes have recently been refurbished.
11 See *ibid* pp 38–40, for details of the expenditure involved in Cathedral Court. Also Bell and Paton, p 230.
12 *Evening Times*, 12 October 1892.
13 583–619 London Road. Thomson and Turnbull were the architects for this scheme.
14 *Evening Times*, 25 April 1900.
15 J Gaff Gillespie, of Salmon & Son, was the architect of both bank buildings.
16 Henry Mitchell, *fl* 1894–1932 was architect. Demolished 1980s.
17 Beattie and Morton were the architects for these.
18 *Evening Times*, 23 June 1906.
19 Advertisement in the *Glasgow Herald*, 13 January 1903.
20 *ibid*, 30 January 1903.

21 *ibid*, 30 January 1903.
22 *Evening Times*, 11 May 1904.
23 Advertisement in the *Glasgow Herald*, 6 January 1908. York Drive is now Novar Drive.

10
1919—1944

Even before the end of the war, the Housing and General Town Improvements Committee had erected an experimental housing scheme on the site of a disused mill on the north side of Garngad Road. There were ninety-two houses in the scheme, sixty-four of two, and twenty-eight of three apartments. This, the earliest local authority housing in the city, was arranged in six two-story blocks, and one three-story block, laid out around a square forming a children's playground.[1]

When the end of the war did come, it ushered in a period of acute housing shortage. Over ten years of complete inactivity in the field of housing for the working classes, coupled with the removal of any incentive to keep the older tenements in repair, had resulted in long lists of people awaiting new homes and a rapidly increasing number of substandard houses. The problem was a serious one and was going to grow more so with the passage of time. The government immediately passed legislation to encourage those responsible to tackle the problem without delay. The Housing and Town Planning (Scotland) Act of 1919, declared that:

> It shall be the duty of every local authority . . . to consider the needs of their district with respect to the provision of houses for the working classes, and within three months after the passing of this Act, and thereafter as often as

occasion arises, to prepare and submit to the Scottish Board of Health ... a scheme for the exercise of their powers. ...[2]

Under this Act, it was estimated that 57 000 houses were required to supply the needs of the city, and that 4735 acres were needed on which to erect them.

Later the same year, the Housing (Additional Powers) Act was passed.[3] This approved grants from the Treasury to persons or bodies constructing houses within the following twelve months. Anyone demolishing or altering the use of any dwelling-house considered reasonably fit for habitation was guilty of an offence and liable to a fine of £100 for each house, and/or imprisonment for three months. The result of this legislation was the appearance of groups of timber army-huts, reconstructed to serve as temporary houses. In Glasgow, 368 houses were provided in this way, at a cost of about £400 each, or about half that of a permanent house of the same dimensions.[4]

More desperate measures were taken in the Housing Act of 1920.[5] To provide workers' houses, local authorities were given power to hire compulsorily any suitable house, furnished or unfurnished, which had been unoccupied for at least three months, and to continue in possession until May 1923. Power was also given to borrow money for the erection of housing schemes under the 1919 Act. Glasgow's first new housing scheme was begun at Riddrie in the north-east in 1920. It was a mixed development of three-story tenements and two-story cottages. The tenements were built in 58 blocks containing 348 three-apartment-and-bathroom houses. In addition there were 271 cottage blocks containing houses of three, four and five apartments, and the total estimated cost for the whole scheme was £1 238 292. The tenements were of brick, with red sandstone fronts, and bow windows in the principal rooms.[6]

In June, there was a much-publicised scheme to provide

HOMES FOR HEROES. COTTAGES FOR DISABLED MEN.
A scheme for the provision of cottages for housing disabled sailors and soldiers with families is being promoted in Glasgow by the Scottish Veterans' Garden City Association. ... A site for the settlement has been secured ... near the public park at Maryhill. For the erection of 12 cottages, each accommodating two tenants, about three acres of land at present under cultivation has been acquired.... Over £8,000 has been subscribed ... and about a third of that amount will be added by the state

subsidy. . . . Lay-out plans of the scheme and the designs of the houses have been approved by the Board of Health, and estimates are to be taken immediately, it is understood, for the construction of the houses.[7]

These attractive cottages are in what is now called Prince of Wales Gardens. Despite much enthusiasm, lack of funds prevented the erection of any more of these schemes.

There is no doubt that it was the cottage type of house, with its privacy and small garden, which appealed to younger people, and this was taken into account in the planning of the next big municipal housing scheme, at Mosspark, in 1921.[8] There were no tenements at all in this scheme, only two-story cottages and terraces. The site was an interesting one with a central hill and the planners did justice to it, with wide tree-lined streets following the contours. After fifty years the place has a pleasant colourful atmosphere and is probably the most successful of the city's interwar housing developments. The total cost for 1500 houses was about £1.5 m. Similar but less successful developments followed at Drumoyne, Sandyhills and Knightswood. Craigton, erected between 1921 and 1923 between Mosspark and Govan, was another mixed scheme similar to that at Riddrie, with three- and four-apartment houses with kitchenettes

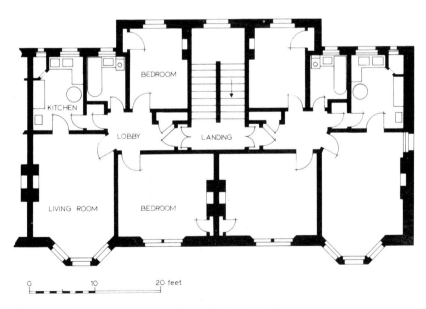

Figure 15 Interwar tenements at Riddrie. Plan of upper floors.

and bathrooms.

Dr A K Chalmers, Medical Officer of Health from 1892–1925, was full of praise for the new schemes and the designs of the new houses:

> What strikes the eye is that a new type of building has been introduced — the Scottish tradition of housing in continuous rows of tenements being replaced to a large extent by the erection of houses in groups or blocks, limited both as to the number of houses per block and per acre. . . .
> But the greatest change has been within the house itself. In all through ventilation is provided for. One-apartment houses have been absolutely excluded from building schemes, and two-apartment houses provided only in those for the rehousing of tenants displaced by the clearance of insanitary areas.
> In all, the kitchen of former days — where the work of the household was conducted during the day and the family frequently slept at night—is replaced by a 'living-room' with attached scullery; and every house is provided with a bathroom and water-closet.[9]

The demand for new houses was tremendous. In 1922, 20 756 applications were received. The corporation admitted that the ideal solution would have been to build cottage homes for its citizens, and a programme of 57 000 such houses had been prepared, but the government vetoed the scheme on the grounds of expense. The idea behind the plan had been to rehouse people of the artisan class (skilled workers) in new schemes while their old houses were to be occupied by slum-dwellers, whose old homes in turn could then be demolished. Unfortunately, this plan was going to take so long to carry out that it became necessary to rehouse the slum-dwellers directly in special clearance schemes. This in its turn raised another problem, for those people were quite unable to pay economic rents for their new houses, and thus began the system of rent subsidisation which has continued ever since. The corporation coyly referred to the clearance schemes as 'rehousing', and rents in this type of development started at £11 per annum, exclusive of rates, for a five-apartment house. Other developments were categorised as 'ordinary' or 'intermediate', and let for up to £33 for a similar house.[10]

The economics of subsidisation were not accepted without misgivings.

> A question that is perturbing many is — what is to happen to municipalities and other local authorities when

hundreds of citizens paying economical rents are faced with the demand to pay rates swollen by the interest on the enormous debts that have been incurred by Corporation scheme houses, let at uneconomic rents? National and local authorities must cease piling up this debt burden which has to be borne so long as the new housing schemes for the masses continue to be provided on an uneconomical basis.[11]

But these considerations were not thought about in March 1922, when the Joint Committee on Slum Areas

... recommend to the Corporation that the time has arrived when action should be taken to deal with the slums, and that a beginning should now be made by acquiring an area of ground near Saracen St, Possilpark, and the erection thereon of two and three apartment houses, with bathroom and scullery. The Committee recommend further that the necessary steps be also taken to demolish a slum area in the near neighbourhood, and that the tenants from the demolished property should have the opportunity of occupying the new houses.[12]

This was the beginning of the city's first slum-clearance scheme, on a thirteen acre site at Hamiltonhill which was purchased for 3s 3d per square yard. The target was to rehouse 700 families from an area in the Cowcaddens. The *Glasgow Herald* wrote dispassionately:

The slum problem is no new feature in Glasgow, and efforts have been made to deal with it since its magnitude was first revealed in the fifties of last century. The war and the housing shortage have made the task very much more difficult, and commendable courage was shown in the formulation of the latest scheme of demolition, which has just received the approval of the Board of Health. The notable feature of it is that it involves not merely the clearance of some 2000 dwellings in Cowcaddens, Gorbals, Anderston, Calton, and Mile End, but the provision of new accommodation for the dispossessed tenants on healthy sites like Hamiltonhill, Polmadie, Belvidere, Yorkhill, and Springburn. ... 72 families had already been transferred from the area scheduled for demolition in Cowcaddens, to Hamiltonhill, ... Their places in the vacated houses, however, had already been filled. That is hardly surprising in view of our present social conditions. We have hardly begun the pumping process, and the only apparent result at first will be a movement of the flood of squalor and misery that has been gathering upon us for nearly a century. There is nothing for it but to proceed steadily with the provision of decent accommodation to replace buildings that are unfit for human habitation. An earnest of ultimate success is the assurance given us that the new houses are not being turned into slums.[13]

The whole question was open, of course, to gross exaggeration, very much in the manner of the media at the present day.[14] An English visitor, William Bolitho, who wrote a series of articles on Glasgow housing in *The Outlook*, took an extremely jaundiced view. Describing what he would like the reader to believe was a typical back-land, he wrote:

We pass through the stone passage to a backland, and come into a courtyard that is no more than a crooked space between the back wall of the street tenements and the front wall of the backland. It is dark as the bottom of a Highland gorge. Growing in the corner against the face of the sombre backland, as straight as a monster pine, is the turnpike stair, a circular stone turret, in the centre of which winds the only stair to the scores of rooms within. Near it is an open stone pent house roofed with broken flagstones under which are three rubbish bins. Cats and children are pursuing their mysterious plans on the loosely cobbled floor. 'This is the back green,' I am told.[15]

His third article dwelt on the impressions of a night visit to a ticketed house in the company of the sanitary inspector.

What deepest misery may overcrowding such as this mean? What ultimate torment is reserved for humanity deprived of air, light, food, money, space? I must answer 'The Slum Smell'. In most cases the inhabitants may not notice it any longer, have grown used to it, like beasts in their cage.[16]

His attempts to find the reason for so much squalor were less dramatic:

There are no great and grasping slum proprietors to be checked and punished by the public conscience. The 40 000 one-roomed houses of the city are owned by a great number of small landlords many of them little better off than their tenants. These tenements of Glasgow are a poor investment.[17]

The second slum-clearance scheme, at Polmadie, was completed in March 1924, when it was formally opened by the Lord Provost. It had eighty-six two-apartment houses and sixteen of three apartments, in three-story tenement blocks.

Each house has a bathroom fitted with a bath, washhand basin, and a water-closet, and a kitchenette fitted with a fireclay washtub and sink, a coal bunker, and a fitment containing a small press. In the living-room there are a dresser and a ventilated food cupboard. An iron bedstead is provided in one apartment in each house, and blinds are supplied for all windows. This scheme is practically an 'All gas' scheme, as, with the exception of the coal fire in the interior back-to-back grate in the living-room, the other apartments are heated by gas fires, and the lighting in this case is by gas. The main walls of this scheme are double, the outer walls being of natural faced concrete blocks, and the inner walls of brickwork. . . . The cost of the houses varies from £286 to £370, and the rents are 28/– per month for the two-apartment houses and 32/– per month for the three apartment houses, both inclusive of rates.[18]

By now, Glasgow Corporation was the only builder of this type of house, the speculative builder having completely abandoned the field. A new Housing Act had been framed in 1923 especially to induce private builders to return to the area of building most desperately needed, but with little success. Two years later, the question of house prices came to the fore at a corporation meeting, for a number of houses were being built in schemes at Sandyhills and Kelvindale which it was intended should be sold. Comparison with the prices of similar houses erected by private builders was thus a matter of interest. A four-apartment house erected by private enterprise cost £875 which, with a government subsidy of £125, was sold for £750. The corporation houses of the same size at Sandyhills cost £650 and, with the same subsidy, could be sold at £525. However, one critic pointed out that, in his opinion, the houses built by private enterprise would still be houses when those of the corporation would be slums.[19]

1924 was the year in which an attempt was made to float a company with the aim of building a garden city some miles outside Glasgow, on the lines of Letchworth and Welwyn, on the outskirts of London. The town was visualised as being built somewhere in the Killearn–Loch Lomond area.[20] The proposal was put forward as a possible answer to the city's desperate housing problem, but did not come to fruition until 1947, when East Kilbride was designated Scotland's first New Town.

Experimental house-types became popular. Flat-roofed houses were advocated, because of the extra sunlight they were believed to allow around them, and the corporation were so favourably impressed by this idea that they ordered five hundred to be erected in their latest scheme at Carntyne. New building materials made their appearance. The Scottish National Housing Company, encouraged by a government grant for buildings of different construction from normal, planned to build 750 steel houses at Blochairn.[21] These *Weir houses*, as they were called from the firm which manufactured them, came in a number of different types, in one or two stories, and for a period were quite popular. Messrs G and J Weir established a factory specially for their production, which was capable of providing as many as 5000 houses per annum, if necessary.[22]

The Calton Improvement, a slum-clearance scheme with a difference, was formulated in 1929.[23] Its aim was to demolish completely the badly congested central area of the old burgh, and to provide new housing in an improved layout on the same site. This ambitious scheme enabled Dr William Gunn of the Corporation's Public Health Department, to comment: 'The slum problem in Glasgow is being thoroughly well tackled now. The slums are being swept away, not only by the local authority, but by the force of public opinion.' He had to admit, however, that despite much demolition since 1925, there were still 13 568 condemned houses, with an estimated population of 37 000 over the age of fifteen. Nor was everyone happy at the prospect of rehousing: 'About 26 per cent of the original slum dwellers, however, had not accepted the opportunity of getting into one of the new houses.'[24]

Surprisingly, it was not until 1933 that serious suggestions were made regarding the reconstruction or reconditioning of older tenements to bring them up to an acceptable standard. The idea was made the subject of a lecture by Dr A S Macgregor to the annual conference of the Scottish National Housing and Town Planning Committee at Perth, in May. Large houses might be divided into smaller units, or single-apartments might be united to form a smaller number of houses of acceptable size. He pointed out that there was a demand for this type of altered house in the older parts of the city, and the cost of conversion was only £100 to £150 per house. He quoted an example of a four-story tenement which had been purchased for £200, about one eighth of its original value, and which the new owner had reconstructed at a cost of £1300, or £160 per house. He estimated that his return would be eight per cent on his total investment of £1500. Many other houses could easily be brought up to modern requirements by opening up for light and ventilation, putting in bathrooms, sculleries etc. In this way, many excellent flats could be cheaply and quickly provided, cutting out the long and expensive process at present in vogue.

The *Glasgow and West of Scotland Property Index* review of the year 1936 suggested that assistance should be made available for this purpose.

> Owners of existing property ought, in justice, to share in a subsidy grant to enable them to reconstruct existing sound property and so bring such property into line with modern standards. The cost of this reconditioning to the community is bound to be considerably less than the high initial costs of new housing schemes. Such a grant possesses the additional advantage, that the important essential of speed would be of inestimable value in absorbing at very short notice a goodly number of convenient and comfortable working class dwellings, and without causing undue tenant territorial disturbance.[25]

By this time, some of the effects of the slum-clearance schemes of the previous decade could be estimated. One district inspector reported, 'It is disappointing that so many leave or are ejected for non-payment of rent; in many cases these families drift back to slumdom and to overcrowded conditions in small houses.' Apparently certain schemes were actively disliked, for example, Germiston where 'out of 492 occupied houses, 140 tenants left during the year, 105 being in arrears of rent. Many from the beginning had no intention of staying, and so took little interest in their houses, and have gone back to the localities from which they came.' Tenants paying 10s per week regularly for farmed-out single-apartments in Cowcaddens, 'strangely failed to pay the smaller sum for the houses in Germiston'.[26] A report by Dr Gunn showed that, in the Calton, twenty per cent of the families preferred to remain in the slum and on top of that, ten per cent returned to their old district after being rehoused.[27]

The question of a satellite town or garden city was revived in 1934, when the example of Manchester, which had purchased an estate five miles out of the city, and built 5000 houses there, was cited. It was clearly with this example in mind that the corporation began negotiations with Sir John Stirling Maxwell to purchase 700 acres of the Nether Pollok estate.[28] Sir John took a lively interest in the project, calling in Professor Patrick Abercrombie to advise on the best layout for the ground. He also imposed certain conditions on the development.

    A The houses built were to be cottage-type houses.
    B There should be ample space for air and light around them.
    C Gardens should be enclosed by coping only, and no railings.
    D For every tree cut down another should be planted.
    E The roads were to be dual carriageways.

Obviously, Sir John had in mind an ideal form of garden suburb, popular at that date. The corporation agreed to these conditions and proposed to develop the estate at a density of twelve houses, or forty persons, to the acre. However, when Sir John attempted to force the corporation to employ private architects to design the houses, negotiations broke down for a while in 1935. Eventually the first sod was cut and a commemorative tree planted in October 1937, when it was announced that 3780 houses were planned, of three, four and five apartments and in various styles — cottages, terraces, and tenements — in about thirty different designs.

There was a distinct social differentiation between various parts of the scheme, particularly between those north and south of the Barrhead Road. Old Pollok, on the north, was considered a better-class area and paid rents nearly twice as high as other parts of the scheme. A typical annual rent in Old Pollok would have been £31 5*s*, while in Househillwood it would have been £20 5*s* and in Nitshill £15 7*s*.

> The scheme will have three main roads converging on a central shopping site. These roads will have twin carriageways separated by a grass panel, and two or three subsidiary roads, slightly narrower, will be similarly constructed. Sections . . . will traverse woodland stretches, and there will also be sylvan walks along the river banks. The two streams, Levern Water and the Brock Burn, run through parts of the area, while the White Cart forms a boundary. The old Crookston Castle stands well within the scheme, and it is to be preserved in its girdle of trees.[29]

The scheme as finally approved covered 746 acres, and was estimated to cost £2 500 000. To continue the policy of creating monster garden suburbs, a number of other large estates on the city's periphery were purchased, but although plans were prepared, work on them had to await the end of World War II.

An important and unexpected development took place during 1938–9, with the building of two blocks of tenements containing houses for letting erected by a private builder — practically the first time this had been done since 1910. The prospectus described the new houses of Kelvin Court in glowing terms.

London has nothing — or will have nothing — to excel the imposing blocks of luxury flats now approaching completion near Anniesland Cross. . . . Superlatives could be exhausted in describing them. Even a cursory examination of the flats shows that the architects and builders have studied Scottish requirements. There is nothing of the 'doll's house' about them. Rooms are considerably larger than in comparable flats in England, and the ceilings are of the height demanded by the Scottish housewife. There is an air of spaciousness about every apartment, and plenty of daylight. . . . Four sizes of flats have been made available at Kelvin Court — 3 room, 4 room, 5 room, and 6 room apartments. The lowest annual charge is £165, a figure which includes rent and rates and central heating and constant hot water services. As one ascends — the building is of 7 storeys — the higher the rental. Floor position and aspect are naturally taken into account. As far as humanly possible, noise has been eliminated. . . . Walls and floors are sound-proof.
The smallest flats . . . comprise a reception room with dining recess, two bedrooms, kitchen, hall, and bathroom. Particularly attractive is the combination of drawing and dining room. The spacious recess provides ample accommodation for dining necessities, and such is the arrangement that this provision does not in the slightest detract from the beauty and spaciousness of what is now usually described as the 'lounge'. In the 6 room flats are lounge and dining room, 4 bedrooms, kitchen, hall, two bathrooms, and two toilets. And each flat, from the smallest to the largest, has a store-room in the basement for trunks, luggage, and other articles not in everyday use. In the event of an emergency, which everyone hopes will never

arise, these store-rooms can be turned into bomb-proof shelters at very short notice.

There are three public entrances to each block of flats, and 4 entrances at the back for tradesmen. Service as well as passenger lifts are part of the installation, with a permanent staff on duty. The tradesmen's staircase and lifts adjoin the kitchen of each flat.

It can be said with truth that these Kelvin Court luxury flats have been designed to make life as easy as possible for mistress and maid. Every labour-saving device has been incorporated. The kitchens are a revelation, with specially constructed dressers, tiled walls, and refrigerators. . . .

All the flats have built-in wardrobes of mahogany or walnut in the bedrooms. . . . Concealed lighting in reception rooms is another pleasing innovation, and tenants can exercise their own taste in decoration. . . .

The same care has been exercised in the choice of materials for the bathrooms. Coloured glass has been used to great effect, and all the fittings conform to the latest and highest-class standards of bathroom furnishing. . . . From the flat roof, on which residents can recline in deck chairs during fine weather, can be seen Highland mountains and a wide expanse of countryside. In front . . . spacious lawns and gardens are being laid down as soon as the building is completed. Amenities also include a first-class tennis court.[30]

This, however, was life as only a select few could have it in 1939. The vast majority were not so well-served. In any case, the outbreak of war in that year put an end to all house-building, private and municipal, for the time being.

In 1944 a restart was made at Penilee, experimenting with a new material, foam slag, a by-product of steel manufacture and therefore in plentiful supply locally. It had three points in its favour — it was quick (only a third of the time needed for a brick building); it was permanent; and the cost was favourable in comparison with other materials. The Penilee houses were built in two-story blocks with flat roofs. Each house had a living-room, three bedrooms, kitchenette and bathroom, with two coal and two electric fires.

The kitchenettes are equipped with modern enamelled tub and sink, pedestal gas cooker, and wash boiler, with ample cupboard accommodation. The ground floor houses have tiled entrance porches, and the upper ones balconies of glass bricks. In all the apartments corners have been rounded [a subtle touch to give the occupants an affinity with their more opulent brethren at Kelvin Court].[31]

Thus, with cheap materials, and clinging desperately to the basic necessities, a new age prepared to be born.

1   A K Chalmers, *The Health of Glasgow 1818–1925* (1930) p 39.
2   *9 & 10 Geo V c 60.*
3   *9 & 10 Geo V c 99.*
4   *Glasgow Herald,* 28 January 1920.
5   *10 & 11 Geo V c 71.*
6   *Glasgow Herald,* 15 February 1922.
7   *ibid,* 1 June 1920.
8   Brennan, *Reshaping a City* p 30.
9   Chalmers, *The Health of Glasgow* pp 30–31.
10 Brennan, *Reshaping a City* p 38.
11 *Glasgow and West of Scotland Property Index,* 1933 p 95.
12 *Glasgow Herald,* 26 April 1922.
13 *ibid,* 2 November 1923.
14 Sensational reporting of Glasgow life is probably best illustrated by reference to two novels — A McArthur and H K Long's *No Mean City* (1935), and Edward Gaitens' *Dance of the Apprentices* (1948). A section of the latter is quoted in D Daiches, *Glasgow* (André Deutsch 1977) p 217.
15 This was quoted in the *Glasgow Herald,* 15 March 1924.
16 *ibid,* 29 March 1924.
17 *ibid,* 22 March 1924.
18 *Glasgow Herald,* 28 March 1924. (This scheme is in Elmfoot and Logan Streets.)
19 *ibid,* 10 July 1925.
20 *ibid,* 25 July 1925 and I H Adams, *The Making of Urban Scotland* (Croom Helm 1978) p 209.
21 *Glasgow Herald,* 13 February 1926.
22 *ibid,* 31 March 1926.
23 W A Horne, *The Glasgow (Calton) Improvement Scheme 1929,* Book of Reference and Notes of Sub Areas gives detailed information on all the property about to be demolished.
24 *Glasgow Herald,* 12 December 1931.
25 *Glasgow and West of Scotland Property Index,* 1936 p 81.
26 Germiston in the 1920s was, as it still is, a most unattractive place. It is north-east of the city, in the twilight zone between Garngad (Royston) and Provanmill, and when built was situated in the midst of steel, gas, and chemical works. Today, when these industries have disappeared, it remains amidst the general dereliction.
27 *Glasgow Herald,* 20 July 1933.
28 Brennan, *Reshaping a City* devotes a considerable amount of space to the development of the Pollok estate, in pp 45–58.
29 *Glasgow Herald,* 9 September 1937.
30 *ibid,* 15 June 1939.
31 *ibid,* 16 August 1944.

11
1945—1990

As we saw in the previous chapter, considerable thought had been given to the necessity of restarting house-building as quickly as possible after the war, and plans for at least one huge housing scheme were ready as early as 1941. However, in the cold light of reality in the early months of 1945 those ambitious ideas seemed hopelessly remote. As after the first war, the corporation turned to the erection of temporary housing, which was dealt with by the Housing Act of 1944.[1] The central authority was empowered to arrange for the manufacture of prefabricated buildings. Local authorities could thus provide houses as a matter of urgency, and were authorised to utilise public open spaces as sites for temporary housing.

The houses were of a number of different styles and materials. Some were of a type already in use, for example the Orlit cast-concrete house, the Atholl steel-framed house, or the various steel houses manufactured by G and J Weir. Most easily identifiable, however, were the new single-story types specially designed to meet this emergency. There were four kinds — the Phoenix, the Arcon Mark V, the Tarran Mark IV, and the Blackburn aluminium house — all affectionately remembered in their generation as 'prefabs'.[2] The first were erected at Hamiltonhill, and occupied in July 1945, with a permitted life-span of twenty years.[3]

The following year was notable for things other than building. Increased violence was reported, and the interwar phenomenon of

Plate 41 Looking north-west from the University Tower over Hillhead and Dowanhill, 1905. The regular patterns formed by tenement developments can be clearly seen from this photograph of an area of high-class housing.

Plate 42 (*above*) The impressive south elevation of Cathedral Court, the first of the two developments designed by J J Burnet for the Workmen's Dwellings Company, and built in 1892.

Plate 43 (*below*) City Improvement Trust housing, Morrin Square, Townhead. This is a good example of the balcony layout which was developed to prevent all the houses opening off the much-reviled common stair.

Plate 44 Annan: Corner of George Street and High Street. This photograph, taken at the end of the nineteenth century and added to the 1900 edition of *Old Closes and Streets*, shows the crowded conditions that existed in the old city even while such schemes as Cathedral Court were being erected.

Plate 45 (*left*) The modern answer to housing problems? Castlemilk. A view of one of the monster housing schemes of the 1950s.

Plate 47 The 'sublime scale' of the notorious Red Road flats.

Plate 49 Oriel windows in red brick: the first stage of the imaginative Woodside development near St George's Cross, completed in 1972–3.

Plate 51 The Ladywell development of low and high-rise flats, erected on the site of Duke Street Prison.

Plate 52 Cranworth Street and Great George Street, Hillhead. In tenements such as these, attractive and generously-proportioned houses are provided on the minimum of valuable building-land.

Plate 53 The Gallowgate looking east from Bellgrove Street, as rebuilt in the 1860s, c 1910.

Plate 54 The South bank in its heyday—Tradeston and Laurieston *c* 1860. In this detail from Sulman's panoramic view, the more careful planning of these new suburbs, with wide streets and controlled building, can be clearly seen. In the upper half of the picture, paddle-steamers

Plate 55   A city being destroyed. A back court in Crossburn Street in 1969.

Plate 56 (above) The Barrows, *c* 1930. It is interesting to note among other items for sale, and presumably 'going for a song', a grandfather clock and a Victorian brass bedstead, both much prized nowadays by antique-collectors! The tenement in the background has no blind window in its side wall, such a refinement only being found in better-class buildings. Behind it is an eighteenth-century tenement with a pantiled roof.

Plate 57 (upper right) Saint James's Terrace, Kinning Park. Working class housing in an industrial burgh.

Plate 58 (right) Women and children, 77 Stewart Street, Cowcaddens, *c* 1910. This photograph was taken in a much poorer area than Plate 55 and shows the 'shawlie women' so characteristic of working-class Glasgow at the beginning of the century. The Cowcaddens was the scene of the first slum-clearance scheme in Glasgow about twelve years after this photograph was taken.

street gang-fights started once again. The aftermath of the war, which saw thousands of displaced persons in camps throughout Europe, had its parallel in the problem of the squatters who, at this time, began to occupy every available building—old army camps, churches and halls as well as private houses. It was estimated that there were 6800 squatters in Scotland at this date.[4]

The policy, begun prewar, of housing the city's population in mammoth housing schemes was resumed with renewed vigour, and work began in the 1940s on Barlanark, the first of a number of linked schemes on the city's eastern boundary.[5] Of the 2311 houses planned, 1944 were to be in four-story tenements. There were to be thirty-six houses for the elderly, and also twenty-eight for single persons, in flats over shops. Communal services were to include six schools with a school kitchen, three shopping centres and sites for a church, library, clinic, community centre and public baths. Among the twenty-three acres scheduled as open space, seven were woodland around Barlanark House. The interesting old mansion house itself, however, was not preserved. In the same area, large contemporary schemes were begun at Cranhill, Ruchazie and Garthamlock.[6]

The Barmulloch estate of 372 acres, north-east of the city, had been proposed for housing as early as January 1944.[7] Definite plans, however, were not produced until 1948, when the Scottish Housing Group, an organisation of large contracting firms, submitted them to the corporation. They proposed to erect 2007 houses of different types, of steel framework and concrete, on 167 acres of the estate. Thirty acres were reserved for schools and 57 acres for communal purposes such as shops, community centre, cinema, library, churches and open spaces. Fifteen single-story cottages for elderly couples were also to be provided. The estimated total population of the new scheme was calculated as about 7000.

The Garscadden estate of 730 acres, in the extreme north-west of the city, had been purchased in 1939 in the hope of immediate development which was, of course, frustrated by the war.[8] Approval was eventually granted for the building of the first phase of this, the first of the monster post-war schemes, in 1951.

> Glasgow is to have, at Drumchapel, a self-contained satellite township of ultimately 30 000 persons—a small town within the city boundary. It will have its own town centre, a central shopping area, as well as day-to-day shops among the houses, and complete communal services and amenities, such as churches, schools, baths, and libraries. The new community is to be built in 4 'neighbourhood

units.'

In the complete scheme there will be 7500 houses, comprising 1500 to 2500 in each unit. The houses will consist of flats of 2, 3, and 4 storeys, maisonettes over shops, flats for single and aged people, and three storey terraced houses. An indication of the scale on which provision is made for communal services is the listing in the units nos. 2, 3, and 4, of sites for 13 schools and a junior college, as well as nursery schools, kitchen, and community centre. Provision is made for a public park and open spaces, and there are sites for 9 churches, in addition to the ground needed for public and communal services. Space is left for lock-up garages in each neighbourhood unit, and for halls for tenants' associations and youth organisations.[9]

It is interesting to compare this description of a new post-war scheme with one of the equally large Pollok scheme, begun before the war and then approaching completion.

When the Pollok housing scheme and other associated developments in the south west are completed they will contain 9200 houses, and accommodate a population of 42 000 to 47 000. Pollok has suffered from growing pains. The building of houses has outpaced the provision of community services, particularly schools. The need for the daily transport of thousands of children to schools elsewhere is still a major problem.... Parts of the Pollok area were built before or during the second World War—Househillwood, Nitshill, and the section of Pollok east of Braidcraft Road—but much the greater development has been accomplished since the war, over 4000 houses having been built at Pollok, 2800 at Priesthill, and 396 at Corkerhill, which was completed June 1951. These new communities include almost the whole range of the many varied types of houses which the corporation are building, including flats at Netherplace Road which won the Saltire Award. Special attention has been given to the provision of single persons' hostels and aged persons' flats, all of them attractive in appearance and amenities.[10]

At first, it was intended that the developments at Nitshill and Househillwood should be separated from Pollok proper by an open space, and that each should cater for different kinds of population.

The Pollok scheme was to be occupied largely by those with higher incomes, while Nitshill and Househillwood were to contain a much larger percentage of unskilled workers. As noted above, the provision of facilities was slow. In the 1940s the whole scheme was served by a single block of shops at Peat Road roundabout, the corporation having decided against a large central shopping area in favour of small blocks distributed throughout the scheme. Such a policy naturally excluded the larger organisations from opening branches, and growing vandalism has discouraged the small shopkeeper, so that a change of policy is now taking place. Despite all the care that was expended on this scheme it cannot be said to be an unqualified success. Vandalism and general deterioration have taken over large areas to such an extent that certain sections of South Pollok have recently been demolished.[11]

Sketch plans for the layout of Castlemilk were approved in 1952. The 1150 acre estate had been purchased in 1938, and the city boundaries extended south and eastward to include it. By that time 6250 houses were visualised, with a portion reserved for slum-clearance. By November 1941 more detailed plans had been prepared for this, the largest of all the municipal housing schemes, which was to cover an area of almost two and a half square miles. Although drawings and models were ready in 1944, it was not until 1953 that work actually began on the site. By that time a huge development of 8300 houses at an estimated cost of £16m was envisaged.

It is expected that the building of the first of the houses will begin early in 1954, and that the whole scheme, so far as houses are concerned, may be finished by or about 1960. ... It is to be built as a township, with 5 neighbourhood units, each of which will have its own shops for day-to-day needs, churches, and schools. In the centre of the scheme will be a comprehensive township centre, with churches, schools, residential areas, a cinema, and a main shopping centre, with various public buildings. At Castlemilk there are extensive wooded areas, and these are being preserved, the lay-out plan showing the township built in and around the plantations. One of the wooded areas will be an attractive feature of the town centre. Some of the land around Castlemilk House (at present occupied as a children's home) will be under the care of the parks department. The old tree-lined drive to the house will be retained.

Provision is being made also to a certain extent for
industry, a site on the west being earmarked for a small
industrial estate to be associated with the new township.
Only light industries will be established.[12]

Seventy-five per cent of the houses were to be of three apartments,
in three-story tenements. Communal facilities were to consist of
twelve nursery schools, nine primary schools, three secondary
schools with kitchens, three special schools, a junior college, thirteen
churches, eight shopping centres, two clinics, three community
centres, library, cinema, swimming baths and houses for nine
doctors. The industrial estate was to occupy an area of twenty-eight
acres and to include, besides a fire station, a bus garage, a Post Office
engineering depot and a yard for the Highways Department. Despite
the twelve years of planning which took place before Castlemilk was
started, its development has been the subject of much criticism. Many
years passed before the full number of schools was completed, and the
shopping centres still only number five. The community centre and
swimming baths have only recently been provided, after much
agitation. The housing-types have changed gradually over the years
and in 1959 it was decided to build twenty-story blocks on the highest
part of the scheme.
    The third of the huge housing schemes is at Easterhouse, on the
extreme eastern boundary of the city. Approval was granted at the
end of 1953 for a township on similar lines to Drumchapel and
Castlemilk, with 7200 houses for a population of 25 000. Work began
in 1955 and the first tenants were housed in October 1956.
Community facilities here too were slow to materialise, and
vandalism has been rife as in the other two schemes, the younger and
wilder elements in the population, unaccustomed to the country scene
and without places of amusement, finding nothing else to occupy
their time. It has been getting more and more difficult to persuade
people on the housing list to accept a house in Easterhouse, and in
August 1972 no fewer than five hundred in the scheme were lying
empty. The situation is similar in the two companion areas.
    These vast housing estates built on farmland on the periphery of the
city could only ever have been a partial solution to the problem of
rehousing. The fact that only 14 000 houses could be built on land
owned by the corporation was noted as early as 1935[13], and a different policy was clearly required. This was to take the form of
redevelopment of the central areas of the city itself.
    In 1943, when housing policy was something of a party issue, the

Progressives suggested a so-called 'treatment area' in Hutcheson-town, which would involve rehousing people on the site of their present dwellings. Multi-story blocks of nine stories were proposed, capable of housing 2000 families. The scheme was fiercely criticised on the grounds of cost and was postponed, being revived fourteen years later to become the city's first *comprehensive development area* (CDA), approved by the Secretary of State in 1957. The area covered 111 acres and had an existing population of 27 000 persons. The clearance of 7420 houses was programmed over four five-yearly phases. The first new houses, in three- and four-story flats, were built in Commercial Road and were ready by May 1958. The next two phases of the scheme contained much higher blocks, which are the best-known features of the development, and will be described later in the chapter.[14]

During the 1950s and 60s comprehensive redevelopment was considered to be the answer to all the city's housing problems, and plans for twenty-nine treatment areas, including Laurieston, Townhead, Cowcaddens, Woodside, Partick, Govan and Bridgeton, were approved by the planning authority. The designation of an area for comprehensive development in fact gave the local authority the totally unnecessary and grossly abused power of wholesale demolition, and its application in the districts mentioned has resulted in the systematic and wanton destruction of much that was finest in the city's architecture. But not only have the buildings been destroyed, but equally important, the community spirit which went with them. What Hitler so markedly failed to achieve in the 1940s Glasgow Corporation cheerfully carried out in the following decades in the name of progress.

The second comprehensive development area was Pollokshaws.

> Lying about three miles south of the city centre, this area contains the old village of Pollokshaws, which prior to 1912 was a separate burgh. The old village atmosphere is still apparent in the area, where, in contrast with other old areas of the city, four-story tenements do not predominate.

The proposals were approved in 1958, and in the following year two firms of private architects were appointed to design the scheme, which was to be a mixed one of high and low blocks.

> The houses will be divided by a series of squares.... Careful consideration for landscaping of the area, and a special provision is made for the White Cart Water alongside which will be paved and tree-lined walks. The entire

development scheme costing £7 m will be completed by 1970. Shawbridge Street will be the main thoroughfare. A square in the middle of the street is to be developed to include shops, with covered walks giving access to banks and offices, and a roof-level restaurant.[15]

The third CDA was at Royston, an area north-east of the city centre formerly known as Garngad, which had been the scene of an early rehousing scheme following World War I. In 1947 the district was defined as a 'Housing Redevelopment Area', and the idea was greeted enthusiastically as a much better and more comprehensive notion than those previously tried.

> This scheme will embody the principle of building in the area to rehouse people at present living there instead of transferring them to new housing schemes in other districts. The proposal is to build a total of 352 houses (217 of 3 and 135 of 4 apartments) on two adjoining sites. One is a cleared site — that formerly occupied by the Tharsis Sulphur and Copper Company Ltd. . . . Then the building of the remainder of the new houses will proceed on the second site when it is cleared.[16]

Work began early in 1952, and it was hoped to rehouse about the same number of people as were being displaced. To help pay for the scheme, houses in the contemporary Merrylee development were sold instead of let.

The redevelopment of Anderston has proved a more difficult proposition than the others because it included residential, industrial and commercial interests. Originally it was proposed to rehouse only about 3000 persons in the area in place of the 11 500 displaced—a very drastic reduction, by any standards. More recently, however, modifications of the plan have considerably extended the residential section of the area.

The most remarkable development in post-war housing in Glasgow, however, has been the emergence of the multi-story block of flats as a serious form of redevelopment. The city skyline has been totally transformed since 1950. Rendel Govan, an Edinburgh architect, had advocated the building of ten-story tenements as early as 1942, for

> If Glasgow attempted to meet the present housing shortage by building two and three story tenements, or flatted blocks, the city would stretch miles beyond its

present size.[17]

As has already been noted, the Progressives advocated the erection of nine-story blocks in their Hutchesontown treatment area in 1943, but conditions at that time precluded the realisation of the scheme. Three years later, as an experiment, it was decided to build five blocks of flats, eight and ten stories in height, at Berryknowes Road, Paisley Road West; but this proposal too was shelved. Eventually, in 1948, the corporation housing committee passed modified plans for three ten-story tenements on the same site, and it was hoped to complete them within two years. At the expiry of that period, however, work had still not begun. Costs, of course, were steadily rising, and it was calculated that the project in 1948 would cost one third more than it would have done in 1943. As one commentator put it:

> This is an experiment in housing which Glasgow has been slow to try. The city has an old tradition of tenement dwelling which between the wars and since has been deserted in favour of bungalow communities. These have made enormous inroads into the shrinking green belts of the city's fringes, and have created transport and other problems that are not yet resolved. Whether we like it or not — and there is evidence that a great number of Glasgow people do like it — the tenement must continue to house a substantial proportion of the city's population. And the 10-story tenement at Cardonald which will push its way skyward in the coming months will be the forerunner of many more, nearer the heart of the city.[18]

Operations eventually began in November 1950, and the buildings, then called Moss Heights, were completed in June 1953.

> By the end of this week the first tenants of Glasgow's newest, tallest, and most costly municipal housing scheme, will be moving in. Work began in November 1950. Since then wages and prices have risen as quickly and steeply as the structure.[19]

The original cost of £2800 per house had now risen to £3500, with a total cost of £85 000. Approximately 16 000 tons of cement were used in the large central block alone, and on an average 300 tradesmen were regularly employed on the work. Walls and floors were of reinforced concrete seven inches thick, sound- and fire-proof. On the south front, aligned to have maximum sunshine, were crescent-shaped balconies, forming a feature on an otherwise plain façade.

Eleven automatic lifts were fitted, each serving twenty houses. The houses themselves contain four apartments, a large front room combining dining-room and lounge, three bedrooms with fitted wardrobes, a bathroom with a heated towel-rail, and a well-equipped kitchenette. Central heating was provided, but in the summer months, when it was shut off, an electric fire fitted in the main room provided any necessary heat. The central boiler-house also gave constant hot water. Cooking was by gas. For drying clothes, a special room with pulley and hot pipes was provided off the kitchen. Amidst all this luxury, it must have come as a shock to those first tenants to discover that all furniture had to be carried up the stairs! The inadequacy of the lifts was further emphasised when it was discovered that they were too small to accommodate either a stretcher or a coffin. The rent charged for each flat was £2 7s weekly, covering the actual annual rent of £50 plus £40 for heating.

In the early 1950s, powerful arguments were being put forward in favour of high flats, in an attempt to counteract the charge of extravagantly high cost which was frequently levelled against them. A multi-story block on a development site, it was argued, would mean no overspill, and that was a most important consideration for the city planners. Already, the question of housing the overspill population had resulted in the creation of the New Town of East Kilbride, seven miles south of the city, and a second New Town, at Cumbernauld, was projected.[20]

The second high-rise municipal flats were planned in 1954 and completed two years later, at Toryglen in the south east. They were also of ten stories, and of concrete construction but planned in the shape of a letter Y. Three houses containing living room, two bedrooms, kitchenette, bathroom and private landing occupied each floor. All electric, with off-peak underfloor heating, each tenant controlled his own heat and water supply by means of thermostat control and meters. Communal laundry facilities were provided in the basement of one block, with two washing machines etc, with a children's playground adjoining.[21]

The Hutchesontown redevelopment plan already mentioned, approved in 1957, was intended to be phased over twenty years and to cost £13 m. A certain amount of displacement of the population was unavoidable; of the 26 000 people living there, only about 10 000 were to be resettled in the area. The four hundred and forty-four shops and forty-eight public houses were to be replaced with fifty-seven shops and nine public houses. Two private firms of architects were commissioned to design the first phase, which was divided into two

146

sections. The part next to the river, consisting of mixed high and low blocks, was designed by Sir Robert Matthew and Partners. More controversial was the other part of the development, designed by Sir Basil Spence and Partners and consisting of two twenty-story blocks of single-, three- and four- apartment houses (Plate 46). These 180-foot high buildings are of concrete and raised on *piloti* or stilts, to allow free passage underneath. Much was made at the time of the provision of a tiny garden space for each flat, which could also be used for drying clothes and which, it was hoped, would help to foster a community spirit among the tenants. The whole scheme was looked upon as a massive architectural and social experiment. An adjoining pedestrian precinct contains shops, clinics, post office, police station etc.[22]

The external appearance of these giant blocks has brought much criticism, and their style has not been repeated. The dark, narrow internal passages are distinctly unpleasant and already, after about ten years, the staircases are similar in appearance to those in the so-called 'slums' they replaced, and far worse in smell.

Despite initial hostility, the 1960s saw many schemes of high flats taking shape throughout the city. The Wyndford development, occupying the site of the old Maryhill Barracks, was completed in 1968 and in the following year won an award from the Saltire Society. It is a mixed scheme of low- and high-rise flats, dominated by four twenty-six-story tower-blocks. Each tower contains 150 houses. These are arranged six on each floor, two bed-sitting-room flats for single people being placed between pairs of two-apartment houses. The idea behind this arrangement was to combat the loneliness of single people living alone, and the occupants of all six houses are brought together in the sharing of a central balcony. It is, of course, simply bringing up to date the Victorian 2/1/2 arrangement, so common throughout the city. The overall planning of the scheme is interesting. The old barrack-wall has been kept, as has the road system, but the feeling of spaciousness is perhaps the most noticeable quality. The scheme was designed and built by the Scottish Special Housing Association, and caters for 6000 residents. Rents in 1967 were described as high by Glasgow standards, the bed-sitting-room flats for example costing £7 10s 6d a month combined rent and rates.[23]

Of all Glasgow's multi-story developments, it is Red Road which attracts most attention.[24] Its vast scale has called forth the highest praise and the vilest vituperation from critics — one of whom only a short time after the completion of the buildings spoke of their 'nightmare sublimity of scale' (Plate 47). At Red Road, for the first time, a steel frame replaced concrete construction in the seven blocks, of which three are point-blocks, two towers, and two slab-blocks. Steel was chosen after considerable research on the part of the architect, Sam Bunton, into the method of construction which would most efficiently ensure both speed of erection and the absolute stability of such unusually high structures. It was calculated that the entire frame of all the blocks could be erected in five months. One of the biggest problems, however, was the calculation of wind forces on buildings of such a height. Eventually the design was based on a wind pressure of 31 lb per square foot for the total height of the building, which in the case of the tallest block is 296 feet.

There are 1350 houses in the Red Road scheme, intended to house 4664 persons at an estimated cost (it was actually more) of £6.25 m. However, within seven years trouble began, with the breakdown of the lift system so vital in this development. It was reported that one lift had been out of action for a week and people had to be carried down seventeen flights of stairs on their way to hospital. Vandalism was blamed. By 1976 the situation had deteriorated to such an extent that a lift had been out of action for four months. The tenants began to complain of being virtual prisoners in their homes. 'Each house is rather like a warm, comfortable, isolated cell,' said one young mother.[25] Even more frightening, however, was the vandalism — not simply broken windows and doors pulled off their hinges, but the frequent destruction of the fire-fighting equipment, and even savage attacks on residents. One recent article on this one-time prestige development revealed that every resident who was asked the question wanted to leave.

Red Road was planned in 1962 and erected during the following two years. In February 1978, after a life of only fourteen of their estimated sixty years, two of the blocks were declared unfit for habitation, and the possibility of their demolition is being considered. It may be added that the demolition cost will probably exceed the £1.7 m paid for the erection of each block.

The second stage of the Woodside development, as well as parts of Hutchesontown and the new housing scheme at Darnley in the extreme south-west, have tried to solve some of the difficulties presented by high-rise building. The chief loss has always been that of the community spirit, which is equally hard to foster in a widespread suburban sprawl or in a multi-story block where one's neighbours may be hardly ever seen. At Woodside, the height of the buildings has been restricted to eight stories, with some of the blocks of lesser height. Many different types and sizes of houses are intermixed in order to include a broader cross-section of society and all age-groups. Connecting walkways at different levels above ground are intended to make passage to and from different parts of the scheme simple, speedy and safe. The architects at Woodside have also introduced colour and interest to their scheme by their skilful use of warm red brick.[26]

Since 1975 attitudes have changed considerably. A belated recognition of the potential of tenement housing has resulted in a more serious appraisal of the city's older housing stock. The public has been given a greater say in the latest development schemes, resulting in preservation and refurbishment in many cases, supervised by local housing associations. Partick, Keppochhill, Queen's Cross and Woodlands are notable areas where this has happened. Unfortunately demolitions have not altogether ceased. In 1980, Alexander Thomson's magnificent Queen's Park Terrace in Eglinton Street was wantonly destroyed, as were three outstanding tenements in Eldon Street seven years later. But more recent housing has also disappeared. After years of debate, the notorious Hutchesontown E development of the late 1960s, much praised in its day, but latterly uninhabitable because of dampness, was taken down in 1988. Selective demolition is also being considered for parts of the monster schemes of the 1950s.

There has been a drastic change regarding the provision of new housing also. In Govan and Plantation, attractive new housing with buildings of varying shapes and heights in attractive informal settings have been erected. Colourful red brick housing by both the local authority and private builders have been erected at Saint George's Cross, Maryhill Road, Monteith Row and Govanhill. A number of inter and post-war schemes have been given a face-lift — for example pitched roofs have been added to the former flat-roofed blocks in Priesthill and Toryglen. Enthusiasm for improvement has gone too far, however, with the addition of pitched roofs to Basil Spence's monumental Queen Elizabeth Court flats, which now look positively grotesque.

An unforeseen development has been the reconstruction of a number of city centre buildings as executive flats. Good examples of this may be seen at Canada Court in Miller Street, warehouses in Ingram Street and Bell Street, but, most spectacular of all, Trinity College, near Park Circus.

Visitors, seeing this improved and brightened city, may be misled into imagining that little or nothing has been lost. This book will have served its purpose if it fulfils the author's wish to provide a balanced

and unbiased picture of the development of Glasgow's changing
housing over the past 400 years.

1 *7 & 8 Geo VI c 36*, The Housing (Temporary Accommodation) Act 1944.
2 Glasgow Corporation Housing Department, *Review of operations 1919–1947* pp 43–44.
3 Despite their success, most of the prefabs have disappeared. One group may still be seen at Hangingshaw, Mount Florida.
4 *Glasgow Herald*, 28 March and 11 October 1946.
5 *ibid*, 15 December 1950.
6 A table of all the larger housing schemes of 500 houses and over are listed in J Cunnison and J B S Gilfillan (eds). *Glasgow* (The Third Statistical Account of Scotland. 1959) p 881.
7 *Glasgow Herald*, 15 December 1950.
8 *ibid*, 15 June 1939.
9 *ibid*, 14 February 1952. A general background to the big schemes of the 1950s will be found in Glasgow Corporation's publication *Farewell to the Single End* by E Reoch (1976) p 33.
10 *Glasgow Herald*, 16 October 1952.
11 Brennan, *Reshaping a city* pp 45–48.
12 *Glasgow Herald*, 22 November 1952.
13 *Glasgow Herald*, 25 September 1935, where the recent housing schemes are condemned as hideous monuments, and the use of ships anchored off industrial areas suggested as a temporary measure to alleviate the housing shortage.
14 Brennan, *Reshaping a city* p 60.
15 *Glasgow Herald*, 25 August 1960. The architects of the northern, Shawhill portion of the scheme were J L Gleave and Partners, and those of the southern or main portion Boswell, Mitchell & Johnston.
16 *Glasgow Herald*, 25 December 1951.
17 *ibid*, 7 December 1942.
18 *ibid*, 24 August 1950.
19 *ibid*, 8 June 1953.
20 An account of the background and development of both East Kilbride and Cumbernauld will be found in F J Osborn and A Whittick. *New Towns — their Origins, Achievements and Progress* (LeGraw Hill 1977).
21 *Glasgow Herald*, 21 October 1954 and 5 December 1956.
22 *ibid*, 9 February 1957 and 28 August 1958.
23 *ibid*, 12 September 1967.
24 Description of the Red Road Development for the Corporation of Glasgow.
25 *Glasgow Herald*, 5 November 1971.
26 Boswell, Mitchell & Johnston were the architects for this scheme.

Glossary

Ashlar   Masonry of squared stones in regular rows.

Astragal   A bar dividing the panes of a window.

Back-land   A building in the area behind the street buildings.

Bed-closet   A rectangular cubicle generally about 6 feet by 4 feet with a built-in bed. When the bed-closet is not in use, and the door is closed, it has the same appearance as a storage closet.

Bed-recess   Similar to a bed-closet but with the front open.

Blind-window   An opening in the external wall resembling a window, but with the aperture closed with stone or brick.

Bow window   A window which projects from the wall, generally three-sided, or forming a segment of a circle.

Brace   A chimneypiece.

Buskit   Pointed.

Caryatid   A female figure or head used instead of a column.

Close   Originally the enclosed courtyard behind a building, later a narrow lane between back-lands or the common passage leading from the street to the back-court, and thence the stair.

Colonnade   A series or row of columns or pillars.

Column   A vertical support with a circular shaft.

Console   An ornamental bracket, generally above a door or window and supporting a cornice.

Corbel   A projecting stone supporting a beam, parapet, turret, or oriel window.

Cornice   The projecting moulding forming the upper part of the Classical entablature.

Coved   Formed with an arch.

Crow or corbie steps   A gable consisting of a series of steps, originally used for access to the roof and chimney head.

Cupola   A dome-shaped window above a stair well.

Dado   An area around the lower part of the walls of a room, between the skirting board and a simple wooden moulding about three feet above.

Dog-leg stair   A stair rising in two straight parallel flights.

Dormer   An attic window placed vertically above the eaves.

Dressings   Blocks of polished, squared stone used at the corners of a building, and around the doors and windows.

Engaged column   A column which projects about half its thickness from a wall surface.

Entablature   In Classical architecture, the section above the column *ie* the architrave, frieze, and cornice.

Fanlight   A window immediately above a door, originally fan-shaped and often containing iron or wood astragals representing a fan.

Flue   The passage in the thickness of a wall to allow the smoke to escape from a fireplace.

Gable (Gavill)   The end wall of a building, usually rising in triangular form to a chimney head.

Gablet   A small gable, usually on the front of a building.

Hanging stair   A stair where the steps are built into the outer wall and are otherwise unsupported.

Harl   To cover the outer walls of a building with cement mixed with gravel to keep out damp.

Louvred window   A window consisting of a number of horizontal bars set at an angle to admit air and exclude rain.

Nepus gable   Small gabled projection on the front of a building usually with window and chimney head.

Newel   The central column of a wheel or circular stair.

Oriel window   A bow window starting above ground level, and projecting on corbelling.

Outshot   An extension of the main building.

Pait   Coping or crow-steps.

Pediment   The triangular part of the gable of a Classical temple, later often used above Renaissance doorways and windows.

Pend   A wide passage through a building to allow vehicular access to the back-court.

Piazza   An open public space, but in this sense an arcade in the principal shopping streets.

Pilaster   A square pillar attached to a wall, and projecting only about a quarter of its thickness.

Pillar   A vertical support with a square or multi-sided shaft.

Press   A shallow cupboard.

Pylonic   With steeply sloping sides.

Quoins   The dressed corner stones of a building, usually placed with long and short faces alternately.

Raggle   To cut a groove in a gable to receive the edge of a roof.

Rigging   The roof ridge.

Rubble   Masonry formed of stones of different shapes and sizes.

Rusticated   Masonry hewn with grooves between the courses to emphasise the joints.

Scale-and-platt stair   A stair formed of straight parallel flights with landings.

Skew-putt   The carved lowest stone of the coping of a gable. When cylindrical in shape it is called a *rolled skew-putt*.

String course   A horizontal moulding carried across the facade of a building.

Terrace   A row of houses, each of which occupies the whole height of the building.

Turnpike stair   A wheel or circular stair rising around a central column.

Vent   The passage in the thickness of a wall to allow the smoke to escape from a fireplace.

Bibliography

Acts of Parliament relating to the City of Glasgow
Adams, Ian H: *The Making of Urban Scotland* (Croom Helm) 1978
Annan, Thomas: *Photographs of the Old Closes and Streets of Glasgow 1868/1877* (New ed, Dover Publications 1977)
Begg, Tom: *50 Special Years. A Study in Scottish Housing* (Henry Melland 1987)
Bell, James and Paton, James: *Glasgow, its Municipal Organization and Administration* (1896)
Brennan, T: *Reshaping a City — Glasgow* (1959)
Brotchie, T C F: *The History of Govan* (1905; new ed 1938)
Burnet, John: *History of the Water Supply of Glasgow from the Commencement of the Present Century* (1869)
Butt, John (ed): *Robert Owen — Prince of Cotton Spinners* (David & Charles 1971)
Butt, John: 'Working-class Housing in Glasgow 1851—1914' in *The History of Working-Class Housing — a Symposium* ed Stanley D Chapman (David & Charles 1971)
Chalmers, A K: *The Health of Glasgow 1818—1925* (1930)
Chalmers, A K and Mann, John: 'Can the undesirable tenant be trained in citizenship?'
. (Papers read before the Royal Philosophical Society of Glasgow, 1933)
Chalmers, Peter M: *The Cathedral Church of Glasgow* (1914)
Chisholm Samuel: 'History and the results of the operations of the Glasgow City Improvement Trust' *PRPSG* XXVII 1895—6 p 39
Cleland, James: *Abridgement of the Annals of Glasgow* (1817)
Cleland, James: *The Rise and Progress of the City of Glasgow* (1820)
Connell, Isaac: *Law affecting Building Operations and Architects' and Builders' Contracts* (1903)
Crawfurd, George: *A Sketch of the Rise and Progress of the Trades' House of Glasgow* (1858)
Crawfurd, George and Semple, William: *The History of the Shire of Renfrew* (1782)
Cruden, Stewart H: *The Scottish Castle* (1960)
Cruikshank, James: *A Sketch of the Incorporation of Masons* (1879)
Cunnison, J and Gilfillan, J B S (eds): *Glasgow* (The Third Statistical Account of Scotland, 1959)
Daiches, David: *Glasgow* (André Deutsch 1977)
Dalrymple, James, 1st Viscount Stair: *Institutes of the Law of Scotland* (1681; new ed 2 vols, 1832)
Denholm, James; *The History of the City of Glasgow and Suburbs* (3rd ed 1804)
Dickinson, William Croft and Pryde, G S: *A New History of Scotland* (2 vols, 1961—62)
Doak, A M and Young, Andrew M (eds); *Glasgow at a Glance* (New ed Hale 1977)
Eyre-Todd, George (ed): *The Book of Glasgow Cathedral* (1898)
Ferguson, R: *The Writing on the Wall — New Images of Easterhouse* (Privately published, 1977)
Gairdner, William T: 'On defects in house construction in Glasgow as a cause of mortality' *PRPSG* VII 1870—1 p 245
Gemmell, William: *The Oldest House in Glasgow* (1910)
Gibson, John: *The History of Glasgow from the Earliest Accounts to the Present Time* (1777)
Glasgow Boundaries Commission: *Report of the Glasgow Boundaries Commissions* (1888)
Glasgow and Building Trades Exchange Catalogue and Book of Reference (1908)
Glasgow Contemporaries at the Dawn of the XXth Century (1901)
Glasgow Corporation Housing Department: *Notes on the operations of the Improvements Department* (annual publication)
Glasgow Corporation Housing Department: *Review of Operations 1919—1947*
Glasgow Provisional Order 1879 *Building Regulations Proceedings before Sheriff Clark* (1879)
Glasgow and West of Scotland Property Index 1933, 1934, 1936, 1938
Gomme, Andor and Walker, David: *Architecture of Glasgow* (Lund Humphries 1968)
Gordon, George (ed): *Perspectives of the Scottish City* (Aberdeen University Press 1985)
Gordon, George and Dicks, Brian: *Scottish Urban History* (Aberdeen University Press 1983)
Gordon, J F S (ed): *Glasghu Facies — a View of the City of Glasgow* (2 vols, 1872)
Graham, Henry G: *The Social Life of Scotland in the Eighteenth Century* (5th ed 1969)
Handley, James E: *The Irish in Scotland 1798—1845* (2nd ed 1964)

Harvey, Colin: *Ha'penny Help — a Record of Social Improvement in Victorian Glasgow* (Heatherbank Press, 1976)

Hill, William H: *History of the Hospital and School Founded in Glasgow by George & Thomas Hutcheson of Lambhill* (1881)

Hill, William H: *View of the Merchants' House of Glasgow* (1866)

Honeyman, John: 'Social and Sanitary Problems' *PRPSG* XX 1888—9 p 25

Horne, William A: *The Glasgow (Calton) Improvement Scheme 1929* Particulars of the Scheme, vital statistics, Book of Reference and Detailed Statement.

Inventory of the Ancient and Historical Monuments of the City of Edinburgh (1951)

Kay, Arthur *The Corporation of Glasgow as Owners of Shops, Tenements and Warehouses* (1902)

Laidlaw, Stuart: *Glasgow Common Lodging-Houses and the People living in them* (1956)

Lindsay, John (ed): *Municipal Glasgow, its Evolution and Enterprises* (1914)

Lugton, Thomas: *The Old Ludgings of Glasgow* (1902)

McCallum, Andrew: *Pollokshaws — Village and Burgh 1600—1912* (1925)

MacDonald, Hugh: *Rambles Round Glasgow* (1854)

Macfarlan, Duncan and Cleland, James: 'The City of Glasgow' in *The Statistical Account of Scotland* (1835)

MacGeorge, Andrew: *Old Glasgow: — The Place and the People* (1880; new ed Educational Productions 1976)

MacGregor, Alexander: *Public Health in Glasgow 1905—1946* (1967)

MacGregor, George: *The History of Glasgow from the Earliest Period to the Present Time* (1881)

Mackenzie, W Mackay: *The Medieval Castle in Scotland* (1927)

McLeish, D A S and Simpson, T P: *Style for Deed of Conditions Affecting Tenement Property* (1948)

McUre, John: *The History of Glasgow* (1736; new ed 1830)

McWilliam, Colin: *Scottish Townscape* (Collins 1975)

Marwick, James D (ed): *Charters and Other Documents Relating to the City of Glasgow* (3 vols, 1897—1906)

Marwick, James D: *Glasgow — The Water Supply of the City* (1901)

Marwick, James D: *The River Clyde and the Clyde Burghs* (1909)

Marwick, James D and Renwick, R (eds): *Extracts from the Records of the Burgh of Glasgow* (11 vols, 1876—1916)

Memoirs and Portraits of One Hundred Glasgow Men (1886)

Miles Better, Miles to go. The Story of Glasgow's Housing Associations (1984)

Miller, Ronald and Tivy, Joy (eds): *The Glasgow Region* (1958)

Minutes of the Glasgow City Improvement Trust 1866—1923

Morton, Henry B: *A Hillhead Album* (1973)

Murray, David: *Early Burgh Organization in Scotland,* vol 1, *Glasgow* (1924)

Napier, James: *Notes and Reminiscences relating to Partick* (1873)

Osborn, F J and Whittick, A: *New Towns — their Origins, Achievements and Progress* (LeGraw Hill 1977)

Pagan, James: *Sketches of the History of Glasgow* (1847)

Post Office Directories for the City of Glasgow

Pride, Glen L: *Glossary of Scottish Building* (Scottish Civic Trust 1976)

Primrose, James: *Medieval Glasgow* (1913)

Property Index for Glasgow and West of Scotland

Provisional List of Buildings of Architectural or Historical Interest — Glasgow (1965)

Reid, James M: *Glasgow* (1956)

Renwick, Robert (ed): *Abstract of Protocols of the Town Clerks of Glasgow* (11 vols, 1894—1900)

Reoch, Ernest: *Farewell to the Single End* (Glasgow Corporation 1976)

Russell, James B: 'A case of overcrowding in Glasgow' *British Architect,* 1 January 1887

Russell, James B: 'On the "Ticketed Houses" of Glasgow' *PRPSG* XX 1888—9 p 1

'Senex' and others: *Glasgow Past and Present* (3 vols, 1884)

'Shadow': *Midnight Scenes and Social Photographs, being Sketches of Life in the Streets, Wynds, and Dens of the City of Glasgow* (1858; new ed, ed J McCaffrey, University of Glasgow Press 1976)

Sinclair, John (ed): *The Statistical Account of Scotland* (1791—9; new ed Educational Productions 1974) Chapters on Glasgow, the Barony and Gorbals.

Skelton, John: *Skelton's Handbook of Public Health* (ed J P MacDougall and A Murray 1898)

Small, David and Millar, A H: *Sketches of Quaint Bits in Glasgow* (1887)

Smith, John G and Mitchell, John O: *The Old Country Houses of the Old Glasgow Gentry* (2nd ed 1878)

Smout, T C: *A History of the Scottish People 1560—1830* (Collins 1969; Fontana 1972)

Smout, T C: *A Century of the Scottish People 1830—1950* (Collins 1986)

Stewart, George: *Curiosities of Glasgow Citizenship* (1881)

Stratten & Stratten (Publishers): *Stratten's Glasgow and its Environs — Literary, Commerical and Social Review* (1891)

Stuart, Robert: *Views and Notices of Glasgow in Former Times* (1848)

Taylor, Charles: *Partick — Past and Present* (1902)

Thomson, Alexander: *Random Notes and Rambling Recollections of . . . Maryhill 1750—1894* (1895)

Youngson, A J: *The Making of Classical Edinburgh* (Edinburgh University Press 1966)

Who's Who in Glasgow in 1909

The British Architect
The Builder
Evening Times 1877—1914
Glasgow Constitutional
Glasgow Courier 1791—1859
Glasgow Herald 1805—1978
Proceedings of the [Royal] Philosophical Society of Glasgow (PRPSG) 1870—1896

Acknowledgments

This book evolved over many years, reaching its first form in 1976, after a long period of physical inactivity following a serious road accident. I owe a special debt of gratitude to Thomas Norton, the surgeon who restored me to active life, and without whose skill and dedication the work of so many years could never have come to fruition. I should like to thank the staff of the Mitchell Library, Glasgow, for their patience and helpfulness, and the partners and staff of Messrs A J and A Graham for assistance in many ways. To John Murray Cassidy I am particularly indebted for his practical encouragement, and for allowing me to share his vast knowledge of the legal aspects of housing.

The encouragement and advice of friends has been of constant help, and under this heading I should like to specially mention Beth and Varick Easton, Mary C Gordon, Lachlan and Phyllis MacDonald, James A Mackenzie, John McLeish, David Miller, Raymond O'Donnell, Amelia Orr, Gerard Quail, and Richard and Polly Thomas. My gratitude also to Scott Gault and Alastair MacFarlane for the line drawings, and to Sam Bunton and Ninian Johnston for providing me with information regarding the housing developments for which their firms were responsible.

For the opportunity of producing this second, revised edition with its original title, I am greatly indebted to my publisher Richard Drew, whose enthusiasm has given the work a new lease of life. Lastly, my thanks to James Murray, who designed it with such care.

Thanks are due to the following for permission to reproduce copyright material:

Dr S D Chapman for the table on p 96, from *The History of Working-class Housing — a Symposium* (David & Charles 1971) p 71.
George Outram & Co Ltd for the quotations from the *Glasgow Herald* in Chapters 10 and 11.
Strathclyde Regional Council (Glasgow sub-region) Roads Dept for the map.

Illustrations

Front cover: Detail from MUSLIN STREET, BRIDGETON by John Quinton Pringle by courtesy of City of Edinburgh Art Centre.
Plates 3, 4, 5, 25, 26, 32, 40, 41, 44, 53: Reproduced by courtesy of T & R Annan & Sons Ltd, Glasgow.
Plates 6, 56: Reproduced by courtesy of Glasgow Museums and Art Galleries.
Plates 11, 23: Reproduced by courtesy of the Mitchell Library, Glasgow.
Plates 36, 52, 59: Copyright George Outram & Co Ltd, Glasgow.
Plate 13: Copyright Colin Hall, Onsite Photography Ltd, Glasgow.
Plate 18: Copyright Malcolm R Hill, Glasgow.
Plates 19, 20, 50, 58: Reproduced by permission of Strathclyde Regional Archives, Glasgow.
Plates 47, 48: Copyright Oscar Marzaroli, Ogam Films Ltd, Glasgow.
Plate 28: Copyright John R Hume, Glasgow.
Plate 46: Copyright Sir Basil Spence, Glover & Ferguson, Edinburgh.
Plate 49: Copyright Boswell, Mitchell & Johnston, Glasgow.
Plate 9: Reproduced by courtesy of the Mansell Gallery, London.
Plates 7, 8, 10, 12, 14, 15, 16, 17, 24, 29, 30, 31, 33, 34, 35, 37, 38, 39, 42, 45, 51, 55, 57 and back cover: Copyright Frank Worsdall, Glasgow.

Index

Plate numbers are given in bold type, page-references to the text in italics. Arch = architect; build = builder.

157

British Linen Bank, *162—170*
  Gorbals Street *118—19*
Brock Burn *134*
Broomhill Drive *120—121*
Brotchie, T C F 1878—1937 *99*
Brownlie Street *104*
Bruce, Sir William 1630—1710 arch
  68
Buccleuch Street *87* (No 14) *47*
Buchanan Street *39, 57, 82—3*
builders *56—7*
building regulations *14—25*
building societies *52—3*
Building Standards (Scotland)
  Regulations (1953) *25* (1971) *26*
Bunton, Sam *fl* 1931—1974 arch **47**;
  148
burgesses *1—3, 15—16*
burghs *1—2, 15—17, 98—103*
Burgh of Barony *16, 103*
Burgh Court *14—15*
Burgh Police (Scotland) Act 1892 *see
  Police Act*
Burgh of Regality *16*
Burnet & Boston *fl* 1890—1937 arch
  59, 110
Burnet, John 1814—1901 arch *58—9,
  88—9*
Burnet, John J 1857—1938 arch **42**;
  59, 115—17
Burnet, Son & Campbell 1886—1897
  arch *105*
Burt, Edward *69*
Burt, John build *56*
Bute Terrace *108*
Byres Road *98*

Caithness paving *32*
Caledonian Mansions, 445—459 Gt
  Western Road *115*
Caledonian Railway Company *115*
Calton **29, 56, 57**; *5, 10, 21,
  83—4, 91, 129, 133*
Calton Burgh Police Act 1819 *26*
Calton Improvement Scheme (1929)
  5, 132
Camlachie *53*
Campbell, John A 1860—1909 arch
  59, 105

Candleriggs *72*
Cardonald *145*
Carlton Place *42, 79, 81*
Carntyne *132*
Carrick, John 1819—1890 arch **21**; *7,
  50, 52, 93*
Castle Street *62*
Castlebank Street *119*
Castlemilk **45**; *12, 141—2*
Cathcart **37**; *104, 108—9*
Cathedral Court, Rottenrow **42**; *53,
  112, 114—15*
ceiling **17**; *24, 40—41, 46, 65, 135*
Centre Street *77*
Chalmers, A K (1930) MOH *128*
Charing Cross **40**; *105, 110*
  (Mansions) *59, 105*
chimneys *etc* 15, 25, 35—6, 71, 115
cholera epidemics *7*
City of Glasgow Bank *10, 51—2, 60,
  96*
City Improvement Trust **20, 43**; *6,
  11, 19, 35—6, 50—54, 58—9, 65,
  91—3, 97, 110, 119* (Act 1866) *8,
  23, 50*
Clarendon Place, St George's Cross
  7; 86
Clarkston Road **37**
Cleland, James 1770—1840 arch *82*
Cleland, J & W (Cleland &
  Herbertson) marbleworks *39*
Cleland Testimonial, Sauchiehall
  Street & Buchanan Street *82—3*
Clifford, Henry E *fl* 1877—1932 arch
  110—111, 121
Clifford Street *100*
close **13**; *28—32, 35, 104* ('wally')
  32
closet, bed *see bed-closet*
closet, storage *39—40*
Clyde, River **1, 2, 54**; *3—4, 7, 16, 22,
  49, 98—9*
coal-bunker *45—7*
College Buildings, High Street *8, 40,
  61, 73*
College Street *73, 75*
Collins Street (Morrin Sq) **43**;
  110
Commerce Street *77*
Commercial Road *143*

Comprehensive development area
(CDA) **46**; *11, 143–4*
concrete *25, 114, 131, 138–9, 145–7*
Cook Street *77*
Corkerhill **30**; *50, 115–18, 140*
cornice *28, 40, 46, 73*
Corunna Street *58*
cotton industry *4–6*
coursed rubble *33*
Cowcaddens **58**; *129–30, 133, 143*
Cowlairs Railway Village, Hillkirk
Street **39**; *50, 103–4*
Craigton *127*
Cranhill *139*
Cranstonhill Water Works
Company *22*
Cranworth Street **52**
Crosshill *36* (Burgh) *102–4, 108*
Crossmyloof *36, 108, 122*
crow or corbie steps **22**; *63–5, 68,
104, 115–18*
Crown Mansions, North Gardner
Street *122*
Crown Street **26**; *77–8*
Cruikshank, James build *56*
Cumbernauld New Town *146*
cupboard, kitchen *44, 46–7*
cupola *31, 36, 87*

Dale, David 1739–1806 *4–5*
Dalmarnock *10, 53, 57, 95*
Darnley *148*
Darnley Road *121*
Dean of Guild [Court] *10, 14–15,
20–21, 34, 36, 55, 66, 68, 95, 97–8,
102*
Defoe, Daniel 1660–1731 *69*
Denholm, James *77*
Dennistoun *10, 59, 109*
dining-room **17**; *39–40*
Dixon, Peter build *56*
Dixon, William, of Govanhill *103*
Doon Terrace, McCulloch Street
103
doors *29–30, 32, 38–9, 45, 90, 119*
Dorset Street *96*
double tenements *28, 30, 34, 79, 81,
84*
Dowanhill **41**; *10*
drawing-room *40–41, 71–2*

Drumchapel *12, 139, 142*
Drumoyne *127*
dry closet *34, 42*
Drygate **1, 7**; *7, 12, 62*
Dunlop Street *18*
dunny *32*
dust-shaft *85–6, 114*

Eadie, Alex. 1823–1906 & George
1836–1921, build *57*
East Kilbride New Town *132, 146*
East Pollokshields (Burgh) *102–3*
Easterhouse *12, 142*
Edinburgh & Glasgow Railway
Company **39**; *50, 103–4*
Eglinton Street **33**; *59, 76, 79* (No
37) *81* (No 355–429) *88–9*
Elderslie Street *96*
Elmfoot Street **12**; *137*

fanlight *38–9, 45*
farmed house *9*
feu-duty *17–18, 25, 50*
feudal system *15, 17*
Fiddler's Close, 75 High Street *5*
Finance Act 1910 *123*
Finnart Street (Howard Street) **20**
fireplace *15, 39, 41, 45*
foam slag *136*
Forth and Clyde Canal *99*
Fotheringay Road *121*
Fraser, Duncan build *54*

gable **23**; *33, 63–5* (common or
mutual) *15, 25, 28* (nepus) *71*
gablets **22**; *63, 65*
Gallowgate **1, 23, 53**; *6, 61–2* (No
374) *71* (No 394) *71*
Gairdner, W T MOH *92, 94*
Garden, Alex. build *56–7*
garden suburb *10–11, 60, 91, 100,
131, 134–5*
Gardner, John *76*
Garnethill **32, 38**; *10, 30, 32, 38, 58,
86–7, 96*
Garngad *137, 144*
Garngad Road (now Royston Road)
125
Garscadden estate *139*
Garthamlock *139*